POSITIVE
LEADERSHIP

Other books by Kim Cameron

Coffin Nails and Corporate Strategies (1982), with Robert H. Miles

Organizational Effectiveness: A Comparison of Multiple Models (1983), with David A. Whetten

Organizational Decline: Conceptual, Empirical, and Normative Foundations (1988), with Robert I. Sutton and David A. Whetten

Paradox and Transformation: Towards a Theory of Change in Organizations (1988), with Robert E. Quinn

Positive Organizational Scholarship: Foundations of a New Discipline (2003), with Jane E. Dutton and Robert E. Quinn

Competing Values Leadership: Creating Value in Organizations (2006), with Robert E. Quinn, Jeff DeGraff, and Anjan V. Thakor

Leading with Values: Positivity, Virtues, and High Performance (2006), with Edward D. Hess

Making the Impossible Possible: Leading Extraordinary Performance—The Rocky Flats Story (2006), with Marc Lavine

The Virtuous Organization: Insights from Some of the World's Leading Management Thinkers (2008), with Charles C. Manz, Karen P. Manz, and Robert D. Marx

Developing Management Skills (8th Edition, 2011), with David A. Whetten

Diagnosing and Changing Organizational Culture: Based on the Competing Values Framework (3rd Edition, 2011), with Robert E. Quinn

Organizational Effectiveness (2011)

Handbook of Positive Organizational Scholarship (2012), with Gretchen M. Spreitzer

POSITIVE LEADERSHIP

Strategies for Extraordinary Performance

Second Edition, Updated
and Expanded

Kim Cameron

BK

Berrett–Koehler Publishers, Inc.
a BK Business book

Berrett-Koehler Publishers, Inc.
1333 Broadway, Suite 1000
Oakland, CA 94612-1921
Tel: (510) 817-2277   Fax: (510) 817-2278   www.bkconnection.com

Ordering Information

Quantity sales. Special discounts are available on quantity purchases by
corporations, associations, and others. For details, contact the "Special Sales
Department" at the Berrett-Koehler address above.

Individual sales. Berrett-Koehler publications are available through most
bookstores. They can also be ordered directly from Berrett-Koehler:
Tel: (800) 929-2929; Fax: (802) 864-7626; www.bkconnection.com

Orders for college textbook/course adoption use. Please contact
Berrett-Koehler: Tel: (800) 929-2929; Fax: (802) 864-7626.

Orders by U.S. trade bookstores and wholesalers. Please contact Ingram
Publisher Services, Tel: (800) 509-4887; Fax: (800) 838-1149; E-mail:
customer.service@ingrampublisherservices.com; or
visit www.ingrampublisherservices.com/Ordering for details
about electronic ordering.

Berrett-Koehler and the BK logo are registered trademarks of Berrett-Koehler
Publishers, Inc.

Printed in the United States of America

Berrett-Koehler books are printed on long-lasting acid-free paper. When it is
available, we choose paper that has been manufactured by environmentally
responsible processes. These may include using trees grown in sustainable
forests, incorporating recycled paper, minimizing chlorine in bleaching, or
recycling the energy produced at the paper mill.

Library of Congress Cataloging-in-Publication Data

Cameron, Kim S.
  Positive leadership : strategies for extraordinary performance / Kim
Cameron. — 2nd ed.
    p. cm.
  Includes bibliographical references and index.
  ISBN 978-1-60994-566-4 (pbk.)
  1. Leadership. 2. Organizational effectiveness—Management. I. Title.
  HD57.7C354 2012
  658.4'092—dc23   2012005958

Second Edition
22 21 20 19 18 17   10 9 8 7 6 5

Cover/jacket Designer: Ark Stein, The Visual Group

This book is dedicated to the positive leaders in my life and the people who constantly exemplify positively deviant performance:

Maxine Cameron

Melinda Cameron

Katrina and Ned Powley, and Madeleine, Edward, Cameron, Elliot, and William

Tiara Cameron, and India, Jack, and Tate Wartes

Asher and Shauna Cameron, and Arianne, Marissa, Cade, and Ella

Cheyenne and Zack Robertson, Kai, Jacob, and Naiah

Brittany and James Gillingham

Austin Cameron

Cam and Melissa Cameron

Contents

Preface

P rescriptions for leading organizational success are plentiful. Scores of books are published each month containing advice from well-known executives, political candidates, consultants, and motivational speakers. This book is different. It explains strategies that can help leaders reach beyond ordinary success to achieve extraordinary effectiveness, spectacular results, and positively deviant performance. It does so by relying on validated findings from empirical research. The book primarily targets leaders of organizations, but these organizations may include families, sports teams, spiritually based organizations, businesses, or community associations. Parents, teachers, and consultants will find this book equally relevant, as will heads of Fortune 500 companies.

The prescriptions for positive leadership in this book emerged from analyses of organizations that have achieved exceptional levels of performance. These include organizations as diverse as a nuclear arsenal, a national health system, financial services organizations, real estate companies, multinational conglomerates, educational institutions, chemical companies, and U.S. Army generals. In each instance these organizations conscientiously implemented practices associated with positive leadership, and evidence of dramatic improvement resulted. Carefully examining these organizations has helped uncover some atypical leadership strategies. These strategies enable levels of performance that dramatically exceeded expectations and reached extraordinary levels of excellence.

I label these strategies *atypical* because they supplement oft-prescribed mandates that appear frequently in discussions about leadership. These include enhancing teamwork, articulating a vision, encouraging employee participation, fostering trust, treating people with respect, changing the culture, becoming more customer-centric, and establishing stretch goals. Whereas such prescriptions are important, and many have been verified as contributing to organizational effectiveness, examining positively deviant organizations has revealed additional leadership strategies that are less often recognized and prescribed. I explain four of the most important ones in this book.

Critics frequently misunderstand and even give a disapproving label to the concept of *positive*, assuming that it refers to squishy, touchy-feely, saccharine sweet, naïve approaches to reality. They argue that organizational life is not a bed of roses, and that most organizations do not even need leaders if there are no challenges or obstacles to address. The relevance of leadership lies in negative, not positive, occurrences. They sometimes dismiss positive leadership as merely one more new age, self-help approach for encouraging people to feel happy.

It is precisely because organizations are fraught with problems and difficulties, however, and because producing dramatic improvements is so difficult, that positive leadership is needed. This book is careful to discuss the role (and the necessity) of the negative, of difficulties, of challenges, and of criticism in the pursuit of outstanding performance. The key is not to avoid or eliminate the negative but to transform it into an opportunity for flourishing.

Positive leadership aims not just to create positive emotions in people—to help people feel happy—but to dramatically affect organizational performance for the better. Consequently, this book outlines strategies that document performance improvements in organizations, not merely emotional effects among those who implement these strategies.

The four positive leadership strategies include cultivating *positive climate, positive relationships, positive communication,* and *positive meaning.* In and of themselves, these four categories do not seem unusual or unique at all. The labels have appeared in multiple sources in the past. However, this book's unique contributions include not only the empirical evidence that demonstrates that positive leadership strategies produce extraordinarily positive performance but also practical guidelines for implementing the strategies and assessment instruments that help determine success.

Each chapter explains and illustrates one of the strategies, provides research-based evidence, and identifies specific actionable guidelines in order to provide leaders with validated, implementable activities that can enable positively deviant performance. Chapter 6 describes a proven process whereby these four strategies can be implemented in combination. The final chapter provides a self-assessment instrument and a guide for implementing the strategies.

Positive leadership is heliotropic. This refers to the tendency in all living systems toward positive energy and away from negative energy. From single-cell organisms to complex human systems, everything alive has an inherent inclination toward the positive and away from the negative. The chapters that follow explain how positive leadership unleashes the heliotropic effect in individuals and in organizations. Focusing on the positive gives life to individuals and organizations in the same way that positive energy in nature enhances thriving in living organisms. The research grounding in each chapter helps establish this fact, and the examples, illustrations, and stories help clarify the research findings and link the prescriptions to organizational reality. These four positive strategies, in other words, are among the most important enablers for producing life-giving outcomes and extraordinarily positive performance.

In preparing this book I benefited immeasurably from the broad expertise and scholarly experience of valued colleagues. I want to express appreciation to those individuals who provided critical insights, editorial advice, and helpful observations regarding the contents of this book. They include Jane Dutton, Adam Grant, Steve Piersanti, Robert Quinn, Andrea Richards, Jeevan Sivasubramaniam, Gretchen Spreitzer, and David Whetten. The production staff members at Berrett-Koehler Publishers also have been outstanding models of professionalism and competence. I am grateful to you all.

1

Positive Leadership

As of this writing, more than 70,000 books on leadership are currently in print. Why would anyone want to produce one more? It is because the vast majority of these leadership books are based on the prescriptions of celebrated leaders recounting their own experiences, convenience samples of people's opinions, or storytellers' recitations of inspirational examples. This book is different. It relies wholly on strategies that have been validated by empirical research. It explains the practical approaches to leadership that have emerged from social science research. Because these strategies are not commonly practiced, this book provides some unusual but pragmatic strategies for leaders who want to markedly improve their effectiveness.

This book introduces the concept of *positive leadership*, or the ways in which leaders enable positively deviant performance, foster an affirmative orientation in organizations, and engender a focus on virtuousness and the best of the human condition. Positive leadership applies positive principles arising from the newly emerging fields of positive organizational scholarship (Cameron, Dutton, & Quinn, 2003; Cameron & Spreitzer, 2012), positive psychology (Seligman, 1999), and positive change (Cooperrider & Srivastva, 1987). It helps answer the question "So what can I *do* if I want to become a more positive leader?"

Positive leadership emphasizes what elevates individuals and organizations (in addition to what challenges them), what goes right in organizations (in addition to what goes wrong), what is life-giving (in addition to what is problematic or life-depleting), what is experienced as good (in addition to what is objectionable), what is extraordinary (in addition to what is merely effective), and what is inspiring (in addition to what is difficult or arduous). It promotes outcomes such as thriving at work, interpersonal flourishing, virtuous behaviors, positive emotions, and energizing networks. In this book the focus is primarily on the role of positive leaders in enabling positively deviant performance.

To be more specific, positive leadership emphasizes three different orientations:

(1) It stresses the facilitation of *positively deviant performance*, or an emphasis on outcomes that dramatically exceed common or expected performance. Facilitating positive deviance is not the same as achieving ordinary

success (such as profitability or effectiveness); rather, positive deviance represents "intentional behaviors that depart from the norm of a reference group in honorable ways" (Spreitzer & Sonenshein, 2003: 209). Positive leadership aims to help individuals and organizations attain spectacular levels of achievement.

(2) It emphasizes an *affirmative bias*, or a focus on strengths and capabilities and on affirming human potential (Buckingham & Clifton, 2001). Its orientation is toward enabling thriving and flourishing at least as much as addressing obstacles and impediments. Without being Pollyannaish, it stresses positive communication, optimism, and strengths, as well as the value and opportunity embedded in problems and weaknesses.

Positive leadership does not ignore negative events and, in fact, acknowledges the importance of the negative in producing extraordinary outcomes. Difficulties and adverse occurrences often stimulate positive outcomes that would never occur otherwise. Being a positive leader is not the same as merely being nice, charismatic, trustworthy, or a servant leader (Conger, 1989; Greenleaf, 1977). Rather, it incorporates these attributes and supplements them with a focus on strategies that provide strengths-based, positive energy to individuals and organizations.

(3) The third connotation emphasizes facilitating the best of the human condition, or a focus on virtuousness (Cameron & Caza, 2004; Spreitzer & Sonenshein, 2003). Positive leadership is based on a eudaemonistic assumption; that is, an inclination exists in all human systems

toward goodness for its intrinsic value (Aristotle, *Metaphysics XII*; Dutton & Sonenshein, 2007). Whereas there has been some debate regarding what constitutes goodness and whether universal human virtues can be identified, all societies and cultures possess catalogs of traits they deem virtuous (Dent, 1984; Peterson & Seligman, 2004). Positive leadership is oriented toward developing what Aristotle labeled goods of first intent, or to "that which is good in itself and is to be chosen for its own sake" (Aristotle, *Metaphysics XII*: 3). An orientation exists, in other words, toward fostering virtuousness in individuals and organizations.

CRITICISMS AND CONCERNS

To be fair, some are very skeptical of an emphasis on positive leadership. They claim that a focus on the positive is "saccharine and Pollyannaish," "ethnocentric and representing a Western bias," "ignorant of negative phenomena," "elitist," "mitigates against hard work and invites unpreparedness," "leads to reckless optimism," "represents a narrow moral agenda," and even "produces delusional thinking" (see Ehrenreich, 2009; Fineman, 2006; George, 2004; Hackman, 2008). They imply that it represents a new age opiate in the face of escalating challenges. One author maintains that not only is there little evidence that positivity is beneficial but, in fact, it is harmful to organizations (Ehrenreich, 2009).

This book aims to provide the evidence that the reverse is actually true. Positive leadership makes a positive difference. The positive strategies described here are universal across cultures. Cultural differences may alter the manner in which these strategies are implemented, but evidence suggests that the strategies themselves are universal in their effects. They exemplify a heliotropic effect—or an inclination in all living systems toward positive, life-giving forces. They have practical utility in difficult circumstances as much as in benevolent circumstances.

Far from mitigating against hard work or representing soft, simple, and syrupy actions, these strategies require effort, elevated standards, and genuine competence. The strategies represent pragmatic, validated levers available to leaders so that they can achieve positive performance in organizations and in individuals. The empirical evidence presented in the chapters that follow is offered to support this conclusion.

AN EXAMPLE OF POSITIVE DEVIANCE

An easy way to identify positive leadership is to observe positive deviance. An example of such performance is illustrated by the cleanup and closure of the Rocky Flats Nuclear Weapons Production Facility near Denver, Colorado (Cameron & Lavine, 2006). At the time the facility was rife with conflict and antagonism. It had been raided and temporarily closed by the Federal Bureau of Investigation in 1989 for alleged violations of environmental laws, and employee grievances had skyrocketed. More than 100 tons of radioactive plutonium were on site, and more than

250,000 cubic meters of low-level radioactive waste were being stored in temporary drums on the prairie. Broad public sentiment regarded the facility as a danger to surrounding communities, and demonstrations by multiple groups had been staged there from the 1960s through the 1980s in protest of nuclear proliferation and potential radioactive pollution. In fact, radioactive pollution levels were estimated to be so high that a 1994 *ABC Nightline* broadcast labeled two buildings on the site the most dangerous buildings in America.

The Department of Energy estimated that closing and cleaning up the facility would require a minimum of 70 years and cost more than $36 billion. A Denver, Colorado, engineering and environmental firm—CH2MHILL—won the contract to clean up and close the 6,000-acre site consisting of 800 buildings.

CH2MHILL completed the assignment 60 years ahead of schedule, $30 billion under budget, and 13 times cleaner than required by federal standards. Antagonists such as citizen action groups, community councils, and state regulators changed from being adversaries and protesters to advocates, lobbyists, and partners. Labor relations among the three unions (i.e., steelworkers, security guards, building trades) improved from 900 grievances to the best in the steelworker president's work life. A culture of lifelong employment and employee entitlement was replaced by a workforce that enthusiastically worked itself out of a job as quickly as possible. Safety performance exceeded federal standards by twofold and more than 200 technological innovations were produced in the service of faster and safer performance.

These achievements far exceeded every knowledgeable expert's predictions of performance. They were, in short, a quintessential example of positive deviance achieved by positive leadership. The U.S. Department of Energy attributed positive leadership, in fact, as a key factor in accounting for this dramatic success (see Cameron & Lavine, 2006: 77).

Of course, for positive leaders to focus on positive deviance does not mean that they ignore nonpositive conditions or situations where mistakes, crises, deterioration, or problems are present. Most of the time people and organizations fall short of achieving the best they can be or fail to fulfill their optimal potential. Many positive outcomes are stimulated by trials and difficulties; for example, demonstrated courage, resilience, forgiveness, and compassion are relevant only in the context of negative events. As illustrated by the Rocky Flats example, some of the best of human and organizational attributes are revealed only when confronting obstacles, challenges, or detrimental circumstances. Common human experience, as well as abundant scientific evidence, supports the idea that negativity has a place in human flourishing (Cameron, 2008). Negative news sells more than positive news, people are affected more by negative feedback than positive feedback, and traumatic events have a greater impact on humans than positive events.

A comprehensive review of psychological research by Baumeister, Bratslavsky, Finkenauer, and Vohs (2001: 323) summarized this conclusion by pointing out that "bad is stronger than good." Human beings, they maintained, *react* more strongly to negative phenomena than to positive phenomena. They learn early in life to be vigilant in responding to the negative and to ignore natural heliotropic tendencies. Thus achieving positive deviance is not dependent on completely positive conditions, just like languishing and failure are not dependent on constant negative conditions. A role exists for both positive and negative circumstances in producing positive deviance (Bagozzi, 2003), and both conducive and challenging conditions may lead to positive deviance. As everyone knows, "all sunshine makes a desert."

Moreover, when organizations should fail but do not, when they are supposed to wither but bounce back, when they ought to become rigid but remain flexible and agile, they also demonstrate a form of positive deviance (Weick, 2003). The cleanup and closure of Rocky Flats was expected to fail; nuclear aircraft carriers in the 1990 Persian Gulf War were not supposed to produce perfect performance (Weick & Roberts, 1993); and the U.S. Olympic hockey team in 1980 was predicted to be annihilated by the Russians. Nonfailure in these circumstances also represents positive deviance.

One way to think about positive deviance is illustrated by a continuum shown in Figure 1.1. The continuum depicts a state of normal or expected performance in the middle, a condition of negatively deviant performance on the left, and a state of positively deviant performance on the right. Negative deviance and positive deviance depict aber-

FIGURE 1.1   A Deviance Continuum

	Negative Deviance	Normal	Positive Deviance
Individual:			
Physiological	Illness	Health	Vitality
Psychological	Illness	Health	Flow
Organizational:			
Economics	Unprofitable	Profitable	Generous
Effectiveness	Ineffective	Effective	Excellent
Efficiency	Inefficient	Efficient	Extraordinary
Quality	Error-prone	Reliable	Perfect
Ethics	Unethical	Ethical	Benevolent
Relationships	Harmful	Helpful	Honoring
Adaptation	Threat-rigidity	Coping	Flourishing

(SOURCE: Cameron, 2003)

rations from normal functioning, problematic on one end and virtuous on the other end.

The figure shows a condition of physiological and psychological illness on the left and healthy functioning in the middle (i.e., the absence of illness). On the right side is positive deviance, which may be illustrated by high levels of physical vitality (e.g., Olympic fitness levels) or psychological flow (Csikszentmihalyi, 1990; Fredrickson, 2001). At the organizational level, the figure portrays conditions ranging from ineffective, inefficient, and error-prone performance on the left side to effective, efficient, and reliable performance in the middle. On the right side is extraordinarily positive, virtuous, or extraordinary organizational performance. The extreme right and left points on the continuum are qualitatively distinct from the center point. They do not merely represent a greater or lesser quantity of the middle attributes.

For the most part, organizations are designed to foster stability, steadiness, and predictability (March & Simon, 1958; Parsons, 1951; Weber, 1992)—that is, to remain in the middle of the Figure 1.1 continuum. Investors tend to flee from companies that are deviant or unpredictable in their performance (Marcus, 2005). Consequently, organizations formalize expectations, reporting relationships, goals and targets, organizational rules, processes and procedures, strategies, and structures—all intended to reduce variation, uncertainty, and deviance. Most organizations, and most leaders, focus on maintaining performance at the center of the continuum, so most performance is neither positively nor negatively deviant (Quinn, 2004; Spreitzer & Sonenshein, 2003). Success is traditionally represented as effective performance at the center of the continuum—predictable trends, reliable functioning, and expectedly profitable operations.

On the other hand, a few organizations perform in extraordinary ways—at the right end of the continuum—but they are the exception, not the rule. They are positively deviant, and this implies more than just being profitable. Positive deviance almost always entails more than merely earning more revenue than the industry average for a certain number of years (as in Collins, 2001). It involves thriving, flourishing, and even virtuous performance, or achieving the best of the human condition.

Of course, no single leader can account for this kind of spectacular success, but certain leadership strategies have been found to enable organizational thriving, flourishing, and extraordinarily positive performance. This book highlights four of these enabling strategies and provides the empirical evidence that supports their validity.

LEADERSHIP THAT ENABLED POSITIVE DEVIANCE—CASE 1

One example of leadership that led to positive deviance occurred in a New England health-care facility—Griffin Hospital—which faced a crisis when the popular vice president of operations, Patrick Charmel, was forced to resign by the board of directors (Cameron & Caza, 2002). Most employees viewed him as the most innovative and effective administrator in the hospital and as the chief exemplar of positive energy and hope for the future. Upon his resignation, the organization was thrown into turmoil. Conflict, backbiting, criticism, and adversarial feelings permeated the system. Eventually a group of employees formally appealed to the board of directors to replace the current president and CEO with Charmel. Little confidence was expressed in the current leadership, and the hospital's performance was deteriorating. The group's lobbying efforts were eventually successful in that the president and CEO resigned under pressure, and Charmel was hired back to fill those two roles.

Within six months of his return, however, the decimated financial circumstances at the hospital necessitated a downsizing initiative aimed at reducing the workforce by at least 10 percent. The hospital faced millions of dollars in losses. Charmel had to eliminate the jobs of some of the very same people who had supported his return.

The most likely consequences of this action would normally be an escalation in the negative effects of downsizing (Cameron, 1994), for example, loss of loyalty and morale, perceptions of injustice and duplicity, blaming and accusations, and cynicism and anger. Given the research on the effects of downsizing, one might expect that a continuation of the tumultuous, antagonistic climate was almost guaranteed (Cameron, 1998; Cameron, Kim, & Whetten, 1987).

Instead, the opposite results occurred. Upon his return, Charmel made a concerted effort to implement strategies that enabled positively deviant change rather than merely manage the problems. He focused on fostering a positive climate rather than allowing a negative one to develop, where strong relationships, open and honest communication, and meaningfulness of work were emphasized. He helped the organization institutionalize forgiveness, optimism, trust, and integrity as expected behaviors. Throughout the organization, stories of compassion and acts of kindness and virtuousness were almost daily fare.

One typical example involved a nurse who was diagnosed with terminal cancer. Respondents reported that when word spread of the man's illness, doctors and staff members from every area in the hospital donated vacation days and personal leave time so that he would continue to collect a salary even though he could not work. Fortuitously, the pool of days expired just before the nurse died, so he was never terminated, and he received a salary right up to his last day of life.

Employees reported that both the personal damage and the organizational damage done by the announced downsizing—friends losing jobs, budgets being cut—were forgiven, employees released grudges and resentment, and, instead, an optimistic future was emphasized. The language used throughout the organization commonly included words such as love, hope, compassion, forgiveness, and humility, especially in reference to the leadership that announced the downsizing actions.

> We are in a very competitive health care market, so we have differentiated ourselves through our compassionate and caring culture. . . . I know it sounds trite, but we really do love our patients. . . . People love working here, and our employees' family members love us too. . . . Even when we downsized, Pat [Charmel] maintained the highest levels of integrity. He told the truth, and he shared everything. He got the support of everyone by his genuineness and personal concern. . . . It wasn't hard to forgive. (representative response in a focus group interview of employees, cited in Cameron, 2003: 56)

Employees indicated that the climate of positivity established by Charmel was the key to their recovery and thriving. For example, the maternity ward installed double beds (which had to be newly designed) so that fathers could sleep with mothers rather than sitting in a chair through the night. The hospital created numerous communal rooms for family and friend gatherings and carpeted hallways and floors. Volunteer pets were brought in to comfort and cheer up patients. Original paintings on walls displayed optimistic and inspiring themes. Nurses' stations were all within eyesight of patients' beds. Jacuzzis were installed in the maternity ward.

Since then, Griffin is the only hospital to be listed in *Fortune's* "Top 100 Best Places to Work" ten years in a row. Griffin is one of three hospitals in the United States to be honored with a "Distinction for Leadership and Innovation in Patient-Centered Care Award." It ranks in the

FIGURE 1.2   Financial Performance after a Leadership Intervention

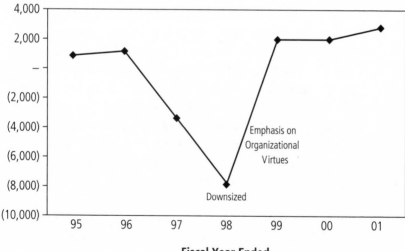

(SOURCE: Cameron, 2003)

top 5 percent of "Distinguished Hospitals for Clinical Excellence," and patients receiving care at such a hospital average a 71 percent lower chance of mortality and a 14 percent lower risk of complications. Griffin also received the Platinum Innovation Prize. As might be expected, revenues have soared. Figure 1.2 illustrates the revenue turnaround just after Charmel took office.

LEADERSHIP THAT ENABLED POSITIVE DEVIANCE—CASE 2

A second illustration of positive leadership is Jim Mallozzi, CEO of Prudential Real Estate and Relocation Company, and formerly a senior vice president and head of integration at Prudential Retirement. Mallozzi was initially brought into Prudential Retirement to help with the merger of Cigna Retirement and Prudential Retirement. He described the challenge this way:

> Talk about trying to merge the Red Sox and the Yankees. We had two distinct cultures—one from New England and the other one from the New York/New Jersey area—and both were very strong, very passionate, and very powerful. As you can imagine, trying to put these two cultures together was difficult.

Mallozzi helped implement a variety of positive leadership strategies and reported:

> It helped us very successfully integrate the cultures. The company went on to produce some record earnings. We kept 98 percent of our clients. Our annual

employee satisfaction scores and employee opinion survey results went up dramatically. We had less voluntary turnover, and the earnings of the company started going up at about 20 percent per annum on a compound rate. It was a real success story. I think that positive strategies helped us create the benchmark for how you take two distinct companies and put them together. (see Vannette & Cameron, 2008, for a description of the strategies)

A few years later, when Mallozzi was appointed CEO of another Prudential Company—which had suffered a $140 million loss the year before—he again turned to the empirically grounded positive leadership strategies described in this book. Inspirational stories and motivational techniques had been tried in the past, so he was not inclined to merely try motivational leadership. He once again helped the firm achieve dramatic results by implementing positive leadership strategies.

We started with a variety of exercises to show our employees that when you start with the positive . . . fabulous things can happen. . . . We went from an 80 million dollar loss to a 20 million profit that year, and we actually achieved two times our expected business plan. We doubled our profits from what we'd expected. Our employee satisfaction scores went up in nine out of twelve categories. (see Cameron & Plews, in press, for examples of the exercises)

In sum, positive leaders focus on organizational flourishing, enabling the best of the human condition and creating exceptionally positive outcomes, not merely on resolving problems, overcoming obstacles, increasing competitiveness, or even attaining profitability. These outcomes may be achieved in difficult circumstances—as in the cases of Griffin Hospital and the Prudential companies—as well as in benevolent circumstances. The key is a focus on positive leadership.

EFFECTS OF POSITIVITY ON INDIVIDUALS

Plenty of evidence exists that a focus on the positive affects individuals as well as organizations. It is largely because individuals flourish in the presence of positive leadership that organizations do well (Caza & Cameron, 2008). Figures 1.3–1.10 summarize the findings of more than 40 studies showing the effects of positivity on individuals.

These graphs merely synopsize a sampling of the findings from multiple studies and show trends rather than provide details. References are provided for those interested in more detail regarding the statistical analyses associated with each study.

These figures illustrate the impact of positivity on individuals' heart rate, blood pressure, inflammation, and cortisol levels after exposure to stressors. They show the effects of positivity on anti-aging hormone production, brain activity, and death rates among an aged population over an 80-month period. All told, the results of multiple studies provide consistent and convincing evidence that positive practices produce positive physiological benefits and, in turn, positively affect performance (see also Dutton & Ragins, 2007).

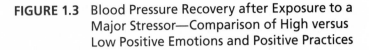

FIGURE 1.3 Blood Pressure Recovery after Exposure to a Major Stressor—Comparison of High versus Low Positive Emotions and Positive Practices

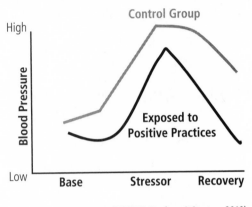

(SOURCE: Dockray & Steptoe, 2010)

FIGURE 1.4 Cortisol Levels after Exposure to a Major Stressor—Comparison of High versus Low Positive Emotions and Positive Practices

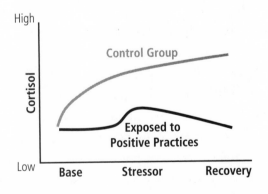

(SOURCE: Bostock et al., 2011)

FIGURE 1.5 Inflammation Levels—Comparison of High versus Low Positive Emotions and Positive Practices

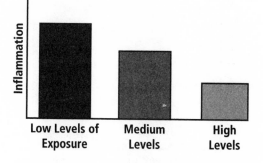

(SOURCE: Dockray & Steptoe, 2010)

FIGURE 1.6 Death Rates in People over Age 70—Comparison of High versus Low Positive Emotions and Positive Practices

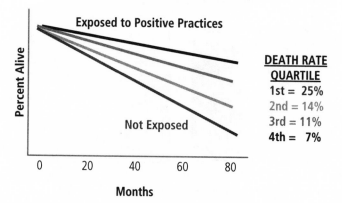

(SOURCE: Chida & Steptoe, 2008)

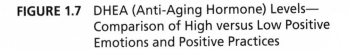

FIGURE 1.7 DHEA (Anti-Aging Hormone) Levels—
Comparison of High versus Low Positive
Emotions and Positive Practices

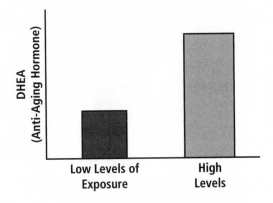

(SOURCE: Van Reekum et al., 2010)

FIGURE 1.8 Post-Lyme Disease Symptoms—Comparison
of High versus Low Positive Emotions
and Positive Practices

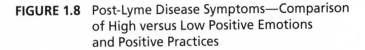

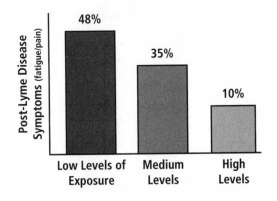

(SOURCE: Hasset et al., 2009)

FIGURE 1.9 Brain Activity in ADHD Children—
Comparison of Trained and Untrained
Children in Positive Emotions and
Positive Practices

(SOURCES: Lutz, Slagter, Dunne, & Davidson, 2008;
Van der Oord, Bogels, & Beijnenburg, 2011)

FIGURE 1.10 Wound Healing—Comparison of Trained
and Untrained People in Positive Emotions
and Positive Practices

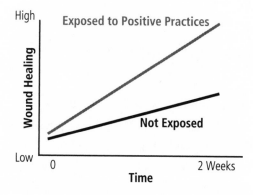

(SOURCE: Robles, Brooks, & Pressman, 2009)

FIGURE 1.11 Four Leadership Strategies That Enable Positive Deviance

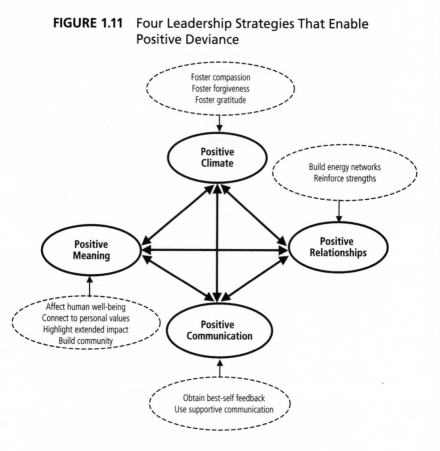

POSITIVE LEADERSHIP

Each of the chapters that follow discusses a key positive leadership strategy that differentiates positively deviant organizations from normal organizations. These strategies do not represent a comprehensive or an exclusive list, of course, but observation and empirical evidence from a number of investigations suggest that they are among the most important enablers of positively deviant performance. However, they are too seldom practiced. These four leadership strategies are interrelated and mutually reinforcing. As illustrated in Figure 1.11, enhancing one of these strategies tends to positively impact the other three.

In addition to reviewing why each strategy is important and how it is related to positively deviant performance, each chapter includes a brief description of some practical activities for implementing the positive strategy, some diagnostic questions for leaders, and some references to the validating research.

Chapter 6 explains a process for implementing these four strategies in an organization—the Personal Management Interview program. Empirical evidence shows that implementing this process as part of a positive leadership strategy fosters marked improvement in individual and organizational performance. The concluding chapter summarizes the principles of positive leadership and provides a process and an assessment instrument to help leaders begin to implement the most personally relevant leadership behaviors.

2

Positive
Climate

T he term *positive climate* refers to a work environment in which positive emotions predominate over negative emotions (Denison, 1996; Smidts, Pruyin, & Van Riel, 2001). Employees with optimistic attitudes and cheerful outlooks are typical of a positive climate, for example, compared to employees experiencing stress, anxiety, or distrust. Well-being predominates over distress and dissatisfaction. Positive interpretations predominate over negative interpretations. Fredrickson (1998, 2001, 2002, 2003) and Bagozzi (2003) found in their research that conditions that foster positive emotions lead to optimal individual and organizational functioning; in other words, to positively deviant performance. Positive outcomes are produced in the immediate term as well as over the long run. In other words, organizational performance is substantially and positively affected by a positive climate (Mathieu & Zajac, 1990).

A positive climate is especially affected by the approach the leader adopts. Leaders have an extraordinary degree of impact on the organization's climate, on the way others interpret their circumstances, and on their definitions of subjective well-being (Diener, 1995; Fredrickson, 2003). Consequently, leaders significantly affect organizational climate as they personally induce, develop, and display positive emotions (George, 1998). The truism is common that "people don't leave companies, they leave bosses." That is, the company may be great, but if the boss is a jerk, the reputation of the firm is largely irrelevant. Conversely, if the leader creates a positive climate, employees flourish and increase their commitment.

Fredrickson (1998) documented the "broaden and build" phenomenon that is associated with positive emotions. Experiencing positive emotions "broadens people's momentary thought-action repertoires and builds their enduring personal resources" (Fredrickson, 2003: 166). Negative emotions narrow people's thought-action repertoires and diminish their coping abilities. In other words, inducing positive emotions (such as joyfulness, love, or appreciation) enlarges cognitive perspectives and enhances the ability of individuals to attend to more information, make richer interpretations, and experience higher levels of creativity and productivity (Isen, 1987). People are literally able to take in more information when they experience positive emotions.

This also builds enduring personal resources such as intellectual complexity, knowledge, intellectual interest, and the capacity to explore (Fredrickson & Branigan, 2001). People become more creative and experimental. Positive emotions also down-regulate negative emotions such as fear, anger, sadness, or anxiety and reverse their negative physiological effects (Fredrickson & Levenson, 1998). Positivity nullifies the harmful consequences of negativity.

In one study of brain functioning, for example, magnetic resonance imaging was used to investigate the human brain's functioning when subjects imagined a positive, optimistic future versus a neutral or negative future. More areas of the brain were activated in the positive condition (i.e., enhanced activation in the amygdala and in the rostral anterior cingulate cortex), and of the areas activated, they were activated to a greater extent (Sherot, Riccardi, Raoi, & Phelps, 2007). People's brains actually work better in a positive condition compared to a negative or neutral condition.

In another study of *vagal tone*—the health of the vagus nerve, which controls internal organ functioning and, consequently, physical health—inducing a positive affect and a positive climate produced superior performance on numerous indices of cognitive flexibility, working memory (Hansen, Johnsen, & Thayer, 2003), directed attention (Suess, Porges, & Plude, 1994), greater self-regulatory capacity (Segerstrom & Nes, 2007), social connectedness, and, consequently, individual and organizational performance (Kok & Fredrickson, 2010).

Enabling positive emotions fosters a positive climate that, in turn, generates "upward spirals toward optimal functioning and enhanced performance" (Fredrickson, 2003: 169). A positive work climate has also been found to enhance decision making, productivity, creativity, social integration, and prosocial behaviors (Bolino, Turnley, & Bloodgood, 2002; Rhoades & Eisenberger, 2002). Individuals and organizations almost always flourish in a positive climate because it produces a heliotropic effect.

THE ROLE OF THE NEGATIVE

On the other hand, Baumeister, Bratslavsky, Finkenauer, and Vohs (2001), in a comprehensive review of psychological literature, highlighted the fact that negative occurrences, bad events, and disapproving feedback were more influential and longer lasting in individuals than positive, encouraging, and upbeat occurrences. One piece of negative feedback amid several compliments, one significant loss amid several important gains, one incidence of abuse amid several incidents of nurturing, one traumatic event amid several pleasant events, or one bad relationship amid several good relationships can have a disproportionately negative impact on individuals and on organizations. The negative event engenders more coping behaviors, longer-lasting reactions, and more lingering memories than the comparable positive event. If a person receives three compliments on his or her performance, for example, but one person offers a disparaging evaluation, given equal credibility of the persons who are offering the comments, the negative statement creates more reaction than the positive statements.

The title of Baumeister et al.'s (2001) article summarizes its conclusion that "bad is stronger than good." People tend to pay more attention to negative than positive events, and for good reason. Ignoring a negative threat could be harmful. From the onset of life, individuals learn that to ignore negative feedback is likely to be not only unpleasant but potentially dangerous, or even life-threatening. It could be fatal, for example, to ignore the honking of a horn or the screeching of tires while crossing the street. People learn early in life to pay attention to information that is negative. On the other hand, ignoring an enjoyable or a pleasant occurrence only results in regret over missing a pleasurable experience. Dangerous consequences seldom occur because positive feedback is ignored.

Consequently, individuals in general—and especially leaders in organizations who are constantly confronted by problems, threats, and obstacles—have a tendency to focus on the negative much more than the positive. They are socialized this way early in life. Moreover, most leaders and authority figures are charged with resolving problems, defeating the competition, and protecting the innocent from threats (March & Simon, 1958; Riley, 1998). Traditionally, organizations require the best leadership when problems, threats, or difficulties are present. Consequently, negative factors receive much more attention than positive factors in organizations.

This is consistent with Walsh's research (1999), which found that positive terms (e.g., virtue, caring, compassion, goodness) seldom appeared in the business press (e.g., the *Wall Street Journal*) over the prior 17 years, whereas negatively biased words (e.g., beat, fight, compete, win) increased fourfold in the same period.

Positive leaders are unusual in that they choose to emphasize the uplifting and flourishing side of organizational life, even in the face of difficulty. It is not that they ignore the negative or adopt a Pollyannaish perspective, but they counter the tendency toward negativity with an abundance of positivity. In the absence of such an emphasis, negative inclinations overwhelm the positive, and a negative climate is the default option (Cameron, 2008). This implies that leaders need intentional strategies to enable a positive climate in their organizations.

AN EXAMPLE OF POSITIVE CLIMATE

Synovus Financial Services Corporation, a regional bank headquartered in Columbus, Georgia, has had an achieved earnings-per-share annual growth of 13 percent since 1999, well above the industry average. What makes it positively deviant, however, is its positive climate. Synovus was rated by the *Wall Street Journal* as the "Number 1 Bank in the South" and was rated by *Fortune* magazine as one of the ten best companies to work for in America for five years in a row. Led by Jimmy Blanchard, the firm prides itself on building a positive climate that, in turn, enables positively deviant performance. Leaders "strive to maintain an atmosphere where employees grow materially, spiritually, and intellectually, and where customers see the culture coming 'from the heart'" (Drazin, Hess, & Mihoubi, 2006: 16). Quotations from senior officers provide examples of the company's climate:

In a social and economic environment where so many things are uncertain, it is more important than ever that the team members of Synovus and the employees of companies throughout the country know that they are cared for. Enabling our working mothers to be productive, valued, and rewarded, while also caring for their families, is one of our primary missions as an employer of choice. (p. 14)

[Our] latest addition, a "customer covenant" adopted last year and carried on small cards in employees' wallets, codifies the company's goal of serving all clients with "the highest levels of sincerity, fairness, courtesy, respect, and gratitude." All of this is wrapped up neatly in what officials like to call a "culture of the heart." (p. 15)

Every person has great worth. We will invest in every member of our team just like we save money for the future. We should build people. Teach them. If team members know their part in the plan—why they are important, regardless of their roles—then their attitudes are brighter. They want to serve. Our returns are hearty. Working here is better. (p. 22)

ENABLING A POSITIVE CLIMATE

A positive climate is not the same as perpetual happiness, nonstop smiling, or constant cheerfulness. Challenges and problems are always present. But leaders who enable positive deviance resist the tendency to concentrate primarily on the negative, threatening, or problematic and instead emphasize positive phenomena—for example, positive emotions, positive opportunities, and positive relationships—in the interest of developing a positive climate in the organization. They turn problems into opportunities. Substantial research confirms that a positive climate at work is strongly associated with positive performance (Schneider, 1991).

In a comprehensive review of social science research, for example, Lyubomirsky, King, and Diener (2005: 803) found that positive emotions and a positive climate clearly engender "success across multiple domains, including marriage, friendship, income, work performance, and health." Both individuals and their organizations function at a higher level. One practical application of this connection between positive climate and performance is the U.S. Army's comprehensive soldier fitness program (Casey, 2011). This training in positive practices is specifically designed to not only assist soldiers in developing personal resiliency and effective personal performance, but the training has "compounding benefits . . . for the military unit and social connections (Algoe & Fredrickson, 2011: 35). Military units do better in the presence of a positive climate.

Three particularly important activities for promoting a positive climate include fostering *compassion*, *forgiveness*, and *gratitude* among employees in organizations. Companies that scored higher on these activities were found to have performed significantly better than others in a study of organizations across 16 different industry groups (Cameron, Bright, & Caza, 2004). (The study included large firms such as General Electric, National City Bank, and Office-Max; medium and small firms; and not-for-profit organizations.) When leaders fostered compassionate behavior among employees, enabled forgiveness for missteps and mistakes, and encouraged frequent expressions of gratitude, organizations' profitability, productivity, quality, innovation, customer satisfaction, and employee retention were significantly higher than in other organizations. Leaders who reinforced these virtuous behaviors were more successful in producing bottom-line results than typical leaders (Cameron, 2003).

Several specific activities relating to compassion, forgiveness, and gratitude can enable the development of a positive climate.

Compassion

In a study of organizational compassion following a major tragedy, Dutton, Frost, Worline, Lilius, and Kanov (2002) identified the strategies that enabled an entire organization to mobilize its institutional capabilities to demonstrate compassion. Shortly before final exams, three non-U.S. MBA students lost everything they owned in an apartment fire. The response by members of this organization represented an extraordinary example of organized compassion. Fellow students replaced class notes, computers, clothing, and food, enabling the victims to take final exams on time. The institution provided free housing until other arrangements could be made. School leaders donated personal funds to help the students get back on their feet. In the analysis of the mechanisms that explained this demonstration of organized compassion, Dutton et al. (2002) identified a variety of strategies that led to this unusual institutional response—the presence of a strong community, the presence of expediters and coordinators, enabling routines that were already a part of the school's operations, collective events, and organizational values that supported compassionate responses.

In supplementing this work, Kanov, et al. (2004) identified the three key actionable processes that enable organizational compassion: *collective noticing, collective feeling,* and *collective responding.* When people experience difficult or negative events, the first step these authors identified is to notice or become aware of what is occurring (collective noticing). This can occur simply by being on the lookout for colleagues who need help and by sharing information broadly. While maintaining sensitivity to privacy concerns, positive leaders can make it legitimate for employees to share personal concerns at work, colleagues can be made aware of others' struggles, and performance management interviews can include a discussion of personal issues as well as professional issues. Tightly knit communities and groups that share a common value system tend to notice one another, keep track of one another, and detect one another's difficulties.

The second step, the expression of collective emotion, is fostered through planned forums or events at which people are encouraged to publicly express their compassionate feelings (Frost, 1999). Dutton et al. (2002) described the public forums and e-mail communication, for example, that enabled compassion to flourish after the tragic apartment fire. The dean of the school at which the students were enrolled ensured that it was legitimate to express compassionate feelings in a public forum by discussing his personal feelings about the victims and by publicly writing a personal check to assist the students with unexpected expenses.

In a separate study of a shooting spree and hostage crisis at another institution, Powley (2005) found a similar set of factors that fostered the expression of compassionate emotions. Public events were held to share personal feelings and reactions (e.g., the president and the mayor organized public gatherings almost immediately after the tragedy, and small groups of people met formally and informally over a period of weeks), ceremonial activities and symbols helped direct compassionate feelings (e.g., vigils were organized to mourn the loss of victims and necklaces were distributed to symbolize the memory of those affected), and personal contacts with victims and vulnerable members were initiated by organizational leaders (e.g., leaders made home visits, shared meals, and minimized hierarchical distinctions in interactions).

Third, collective responding occurs when organized action is taken to foster healing and restoration. Dutton and colleagues' (2002) and Powley's (2005) studies investigated the processes that are used in organizations to enable compassion in the face of traumatic events, and the exemplary actions of the leader were found to be crucial. In their investigations, leaders visibly called others to action, shared stories of caring, and articulated values, in which "we care for our own" and "the whole person matters here," were predominant. Making resources available for compassionate action—for example, collecting goods for those who lost possessions, replacing course notes for students who had theirs destroyed, and rededicating the building where the tragedy occurred—was a vitally important leadership activity that enabled collective compassion.

Forgiveness

Forgiveness becomes relevant in organizations when harmful or hurtful events occur—for example, downsizing and cutbacks, difficult union negotiations, or embarrassing mistakes. These may be major or minor offenses, but in order to move forward and not be weighed down by animosity and grudge holding, forgiveness must be fostered. Inevitably, when plants close, when layoffs are announced, when unethical decisions are made, when trust is violated, or when personal affronts are encountered, individuals have one of three alternatives (Bright, 2006): (1) hold a grudge and seek retaliation, (2) neutralize the angry or judgmental feelings and abandon hostility, or (3) actively replace negative with positive feelings. A positive climate enabling positive deviance is most closely associated with the third alternative.

A quotation from the Nobel Laureate Desmond Tutu (1998: xiii, 1999: 155) summarizes this relationship best:

> In forgiving, people are not asked to forget. On the contrary, it is important to remember, so that we should not let such atrocities happen again. Forgiveness does

not mean condoning what has been done. It means taking what happened seriously and not minimizing it; drawing out the sting in the memory that threatens to poison our entire existence. It involves trying to understand the perpetrators and so have empathy, to try to stand in their shoes and appreciate the sort of pressures and influences that might have conditioned them. . . . Forgiving means abandoning your right to pay back the perpetrator in his own coin, but it is a loss that liberates the victim. . . . We will always need a process of forgiveness and reconciliation to deal with those unfortunate yet all too human breaches in relationships. They are an inescapable characteristic of the human condition. . . . Ultimately, you discover that without forgiveness, there is no future. We recognize that the past cannot be remade through punishment. . . . There is no point in exacting vengeance now, knowing that it will be the cause for future vengeance by the offspring of those we punish. Vengeance leads only to revenge. Vengeance destroys those it claims and those who become intoxicated with it . . . therefore, forgiveness is an absolute necessity for continued human existence.

Based on a variety of investigations of forgiveness in organizations (Bright, 2006; Cameron & Caza, 2002; McCullough, Pargament, & Thoreson, 2000; Worthington, 1998), at least five leadership activities were found to enable organizational forgiveness:

(1) Acknowledge the trauma, harm, or injustice that organization members have experienced, but then define these occurrences as an opportunity to move forward

toward a new goal. Clarify a positive future with greater emphasis than a negative past.

(2) Associate the outcomes of the organization (e.g., its products, services, and relationships) with a higher purpose that provides personal significance for organization members—something they care deeply about. This higher purpose replaces a focus on self (e.g., retribution, self-pity) with a focus on an elevating objective. Selfishness and victimization are replaced by an opportunity to contribute value to someone or something else.

(3) Maintain high standards and communicate the fact that forgiveness is not synonymous with tolerance for error, lowered expectations, forgetting the offense, or minimizing the consequences from harm. Forgiveness enables excellence by refusing to dwell on the negative. It counters the tendency to dwell on mistakes and problems and, instead, points toward a higher standard. Working on mistakes usually produces competence—the midpoint in Figure 1.1 in Chapter 1—but focusing on forgiveness and high standards frees up individuals and organizations to become positively deviant—the right side of Figure 1.1.

(4) Provide support to individuals by communicating that human development and human welfare are as important in the organization's priorities as the financial bottom line. Instead of isolating or abandoning offenders or ignoring victims, offer social support to help humanize the harmful event. People can forgive people more than they can forgive events. This kind of support helps both perpetrators and victims find a way to move past the injury.

(5) Pay attention to language, so that terms such as rec-onciliation, compassion, humility, courage, and love are acceptable in the organization's vocabulary. Such language provides a context in which forgiveness is seen as a legiti-mate response to harm or offense. Expressions of forgive-ness are almost always accompanied by statements about caring, humility, reconciliation, and love for others.

Research on several organizations' successful turn-arounds after the trauma of downsizing reveals that these five strategies were successful in helping organizations move past the damaging effects of job loss (Cameron & Caza, 2002). Abundant evidence indicates that most orga-nizations deteriorate after downsizing, but of the few that flourish, institutionalized forgiveness is a key enabler (Bright, Cameron, & Caza, 2006).

Gratitude

Observing acts of compassion and forgiveness—not to mention being the recipient of them—creates a sense of gratitude in people. Gratitude has been found to have dra-matic effects on individual and group performance. For example, Emmons (2003) induced feelings of gratitude in students by assigning them to keep journals as part of a semester-long experiment. Some of the students were re-quired to keep "gratitude journals" on a daily or weekly basis. They wrote down events or incidents that happened during the day (or week) for which they were grateful. Other students were assigned to write down events or inci-dents that were frustrating, and still other students were assigned to write down events or incidents that were merely neutral.

The students who kept gratitude journals, compared to frustrated students and neutral students, experienced fewer physical symptoms such as headaches and colds; felt better about their lives as a whole; were more optimistic about the coming week; had higher states of alertness, attentiveness, determination, and energy; reported fewer hassles in their lives; engaged in more helping behavior toward other people; experienced better sleep quality; and had a sense of being more connected to others. In addition, they were absent and tardy less often and had higher grade point averages. Feelings of gratitude had significant impact on student classroom performance as well as on their personal lives.

Figure 2.1 illustrates one reason such positive results occur. Individuals experiencing gratitude demonstrate a more consistent and healthy heart rhythm than individuals experiencing frustration. Physiological health, cognitive functioning, and performance at work are substantially higher when gratitude is fostered, at least partly because of the harmonious pattern adopted by the body.

Emmons (2003) also found that expressions of gratitude by one person tended to motivate others to express gratitude, so a self-perpetuating, virtuous cycle occurred when gratitude was expressed. Gratitude elicited positive behavior on the part of other people (e.g., they were more likely to loan money or provide compassionate support) as well as reciprocal behavior. For example, a handwritten "thank

FIGURE 2.1 Heart Rhythms in Gratitude and Frustration
Conditions

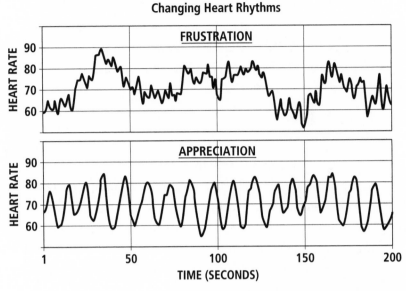

Changing Heart Rhythms

(SOURCE: McCraty & Childre, 2004)

you" on a restaurant bill by the server elicited about 11
percent higher tips, and visits by case workers and social
workers were 80 percent higher if they were thanked for
coming (McCullough, Emmons, & Tsang, 2002).

Engaging in gratitude visits (e.g., simply visiting another person in order to express gratitude), writing gratitude letters (e.g., sharing feelings of thanks with another
person), keeping gratitude journals (e.g., writing down three
things daily for which you are grateful), and distributing

daily gratitude cards (e.g., handing out five written expressions of appreciation to coworkers each day) all have been shown in empirical investigations to produce important impacts on individuals and organizations (see Seligman, Steen, Park, & Peterson, 2005). Despite being easy to implement, their effects are powerful and significant.

SUMMARY

Leadership strategies that help engender a positive climate in organizations include modeling and encouraging acts of compassion (noticing, feeling, and responding), encouraging collective forgiveness (acknowledging harm, identifying purpose, maintaining standards, providing support, using appropriate language), and encouraging expressions of gratitude (visits, letters, journals, cards). Such virtuous acts tend to create a climate in which people are cared for, supported, and encouraged to flourish. As confirmed by empirical studies, these activities are associated with positive physiological, mental, emotional, and organizational effects.

Demonstrating compassion, forgiveness, and gratitude produces a positive climate, and people demonstrate significantly higher performance at work when a positive climate exists. Moreover, organizational performance tends to flourish in the presence of this kind of environment (Rhoades & Eisenberger, 2002).

ASSESSING POSITIVE LEADERSHIP ACTIVITIES

As a quick assessment of practical leadership activities that enable a positive climate, the following diagnostic questions may be helpful. Use the following scale to respond.

**1 — Never 2 — Seldom 3 — Sometimes
4 — Frequently 5 — Always**

As a leader, to what extent do you:

_____ Foster information sharing so that people become aware of colleagues' difficulties and, therefore, can express compassion?

_____ Encourage the public expression of compassion by sponsoring formal events to communicate emotional support?

_____ Demonstrate forgiveness for mistakes and errors rather than punish perpetrators or hold grudges?

_____ Provide support and development as an indicator of forgiveness for individuals who have blundered?

_____ Express gratitude to multiple employees each day?

_____ Make gratitude visits and the distribution of gratitude notes a daily practice?

3

Positive Relationships

ositive relationships are those that are "a generative source of enrichment, vitality, and learning" for both individuals and organizations (Dutton & Ragins, 2007: 5). This implies more than people merely getting along with one another or avoiding toxicity in their interactions. It means that positive relationships promote positively deviant outcomes physiologically, psychologically, emotionally, and organizationally. It is commonly understood that positive relationships are satisfying and preferred by people, but the benefits extend well beyond just providing a pleasant experience. Flourishing individuals are a prerequisite to flourishing organizations.

For example, Heaphy and Dutton (2008) reviewed the literature on the association between positive relationships and physiological health. They reported abundant evidence that links the positive effects of social relationships with social phenomena such as career mobility (Burt, 1992), mentoring and resource acquisition (Kram, 1985), power (Ibarra, 1993), and social capital (Baker, 2000). Studies also have shown that social relationships have positive effects on longevity and recovery from illness (Ryff & Singer, 2001). That is, positive social relationships—the uplifting connections associated with individuals' interpersonal interactions—have beneficial effects on a variety of aspects of human behavior and health.

Heaphy and Dutton (2008) helped explain the mechanisms for *why* these positive outcomes occur. Specifically, positive social relationships affect the *hormonal, cardiovascular,* and *immune* systems of the body, thus enhancing health, well-being, and the nature of the relationships themselves.

HORMONAL SYSTEM

More specifically, when people experience positive relationships with others, oxytocin (a health-enhancing hormone) is released in the body, leading to lower blood pressure and heart rate and an enhanced ability to handle stress calmly (Ryff, Singer, Wing, & Love, 2001; Taylor, 2002). Positive social contacts lessen the allostatic load (the physiological reaction in the body to stress), so the body works less hard to cope under the effects of stressful conditions (Epel, McEwen, & Ickovics, 1998). The increase in anabolic hormones (for instance, oxytocin) associated with positive relationships also has a calming effect on the body and mind (Seeman, 2001).

In addition, increases in oxytocin cause people to seek social contact with others (Taylor, 2002), so that a virtuous cycle of positive social interactions is created. Kosfeld, Heinrichs, Zak, Fischbacher, and Fehr (2005: 673) found that exposure to oxytocin "causes a substantial increase in trust among humans," so that positive social interactions, teamwork, and prosocial (e.g., helping) behavior all are enhanced.

Kiecolt-Glaser, Bane, Glaser, and Malarkey (2003) found that the hormonal effects of positive relationships also have a long-term impact on marriages. In one study, married couples were asked to discuss a stressful topic in their relationship, and four stress-related hormones (e.g., ACTH, or the adrenocorticotropic hormone) were measured over a 24-hour period. Ten years later, these couples were studied again, and it was found that the hormonal levels in the original experiment significantly predicted their marital status (married, divorced, separated). Those with elevated stress-hormone levels in the original study were less likely to still be married. The release of good hormones (e.g., oxytocin) and the decrease of bad hormones (e.g., ACTH) predicted relationship durability (see Heaphy & Dutton, 2008).

CARDIOVASCULAR SYSTEM

Similar results were found regarding the effects of positive relationships on the cardiovascular system. People who experience positive relationships (as opposed to ambivalent or negative relationships) experience lower blood pressure, systolic heart rate, and diastolic heart rate (Holt-Lunstad, et al., 2003). When encountering stressful events, people's cardiovascular systems worked less hard (as evidenced by lower heart rates and blood pressure) when they were in positive relationships or felt social support at work (Brondolo et al., 2003; Unden, Orth-Gomer, & Elofsson, 1991). Social and emotional support at work (especially from supervisors and coworkers) had a direct effect on lowering heart rate and blood pressure (Karlin, Brondolo, & Schwartz, 2003). People simply have healthier cardiovascular systems when experiencing positive social relationships.

Especially interesting was an investigation of caregivers for Alzheimer's patients. In this investigation caregivers with high levels of social support had heart rate patterns associated with a lower chronological age compared to caregivers with low levels of social support (Uchino, Kiecolt-Glaser, & Cacioppo, 1992). Those with positive relationships were not as physiologically old as those without positive relationships.

In addition, a study of 10,000 Israeli men (Medalie & Goldbourt, 1976) found that among those experiencing high levels of stress, those who had a loving and supportive wife had half the rate of angina pectoris (chest pain). After a heart attack, the presence of social and emotional support doubled the chances of survival six months later (Berkman, Leo-Summers, & Horowitz, 2002) and was more predictive of physiological health than chronological age. People in positive relationships tend to have younger and healthier cardiovascular systems than others.

IMMUNE SYSTEM

Heaphy and Dutton's (2008) third factor—the immune system—is also positively affected by positive relationships. Individuals in positive relationships had greater resistance to upper respiratory infections (Cohen, et al., 1997), and men who reported greater satisfaction with their social support system had lower levels of a prostate-specific antigen that indicates various prostate diseases. Positive relationships actually enhanced the body's ability to fight off cancer (Stone, Mezzacappa, Donatone, & Gonder, 1999). Medical students who reported higher levels of social support had stronger immune responses to hepatitis B vaccines than those with less social support, and stronger immunity responses were detected in caregivers who experienced higher levels of social support (Esterling, Kiecolt-Glaser, Bodnar, & Glaser, 1994). These immune responses were due primarily to the presence of natural killer (NK) cells and T lymphocytes that fight off colds and disease.

OTHER SYSTEMS

In addition to the physiological effects of positive relationships, a variety of psychological, emotional, and organizational benefits have also been uncovered in research. For example, positive relationships:

- enhance the emotional carrying capacity of individuals (i.e., their ability to experience a broad range and intensity of emotions) (Heaphy, 2007);

- foster greater resiliency and an ability to adapt to and bounce back from difficult experiences (Dutton & Heaphy, 2003);

- create stronger self-identity and more accurate self-assessments (Roberts, 2007);

- produce greater degrees of creativity, trust, and openness to new ideas (Pratt & Dirks, 2007);

- cultivate higher levels of mutual benefit (Blatt & Camden, 2007);

- foster healthier team functioning (Ancona & Isaacs, 2007);

- raise levels of commitment to the organization (Kahn, 2007);

- create higher levels of energy, learning, cooperation, resource utilization, cost reduction, time savings, and human capital development in organizations (Baker & Dutton, 2007); and

- engender higher levels of project performance in organizations (Baker, Cross, & Parker, 2003).

In sum, because of their association with very basic physiological and social processes, positive and supportive relationships have positive effects on individuals' functioning and, consequently, on their performance (Dutton & Ragins, 2007). These effects help explain the oft-cited finding of the Gallup organization, that to have a best friend at work predicts higher performance in teams and organizations (Clifton & Harter, 2003). Leaders who enable positive deviance in organizations, therefore, invest in the formation of positive interpersonal relationships at work.

ENABLING POSITIVE RELATIONSHIPS

Fostering the formation of positive relationships in organizations is a topic that has been well examined. For example, a search for the phrase "relationships at work" on Amazon.com results in approximately 100,000 books. Forming close friendships at work, it has been found, tends to enhance and increase productivity and performance (Buckingham & Clifton, 2001; Dutton, 2003; Lawler, 2003). Research by Jehn and Shah (1997), for example, found that friendship groups (people in positive social relationships) significantly outperformed acquaintance groups on both decision-making and motor tasks.

One of the most important findings associated with this research, however, is the explanation for *why* positive relationships produce these desirable outcomes. The most common assumption is that when people *receive* love, support, and encouragement, when their psychological and emotional needs are met, they tend to feel secure and to feel valued, and their performance is therefore elevated. What has actually been found, however, is that what people *give* to a relationship, rather than what they *receive* from a relationship, accounts for the positive effects (Brown & Brown, 2006; Brown, Nesse, Vinokur, & Smith, 2003; Grant, Dutton, & Russo, 2008).

Although it is clear that positive relationships are advantageous to psychological, emotional, and physical health, research has revealed that the contributions made to others are what account for the advantages. The demonstration of altruism, compassion, forgiveness, and kindness was found to be necessary for positive relationships to have their maximum positive impact on well-being and performance.

In one study, for example, widows who provided instrumental support to others had no depression six months after the loss of a spouse compared to substantial and lasting depression among those who merely received support but did not provide it. No "receiving support" factors were positively correlated with an absence of depression, but "giving support" factors were (Brown, Nesse, Vinokur, & Smith, 2003). In another study, employees who participated in programs in which they provided support to fellow employees, rather than received support, substantially increased their commitment to the organization as well as their inclination toward prosocial behaviors. Giving, rather than receiving, was the key enabler (Grant, Dutton, & Russo, 2008).

A large number of activities exist for fostering positive relationships at work (e.g., Dutton & Ragins, 2007), so the discussion that follows highlights some less common but very potent ones. Two especially important activities that have emerged from research on positively deviant performance include building *positive-energy networks* and reinforcing individuals' *strengths.*

Positive-energy networks

Research by Baker, Cross, and Wooten (2003) discovered that individuals can be identified as "positive energizers" or "negative energizers," and that the difference has important implications. Positive energizers create and support vitality in others. They uplift and boost people. Interacting with positive energizers leaves others feeling elevated and motivated. Positive energizers have been found to be optimistic, heedful, trustworthy, and unselfish. Interacting with them builds energy in people and is an inspiring experience.

In contrast, negative energizers deplete the good feelings and enthusiasm of others. They sap strength from and weaken people. They leave others feeling exhausted and diminished. Negative energizers have been found to be critical, inflexible, selfish, and undependable (Baker, Cross, & Parker, 2003).

Most importantly, positive energizing is a learned behavior. It is not a personality attribute, inherent charisma, or physical attractiveness. The correlation between positive energy and the personality factor *extraversion/introversion*, for example, is low and statistically insignificant

(Baker, Cross, & Parker, 2003). Positive energy is not a matter of merely being gregarious or outgoing. People learn how to become positive energizers. It is not an inherent attribute.

Positive energizers benefit their organizations not only by performing better themselves but also by enabling others to perform better. For example, in studies of network maps in organizations comparing people's position in information networks (i.e., who obtains information from whom), influence networks (i.e., who influences whom), and positive-energy networks (i.e., who energizes whom) revealed that a person's position in the energy network is far more predictive of success than her or his position in information or influence networks (Baker, 2004). Being a positive energizer made individuals four times more likely to succeed than being at the center of an information or influence network.

Moreover, this success was conveyed to those interacting with the energizer (Baker, Cross, & Wooten, 2003). Positive energizers helped others become better energizers. Baker (2004) found, in fact, that high-performing organizations have three times more positive energizers than average organizations. This is understandable inasmuch as the strength of the interpersonal relationships that are formed, the coordination and collaboration that occur among individuals, and the efficiency of the work that is done all are positively affected by individuals who exude positive energy (Baker, Cross, & Parker, 2003).

The positive energy of leaders is especially important in affecting organizations' and employees' performance.

Figures 3.1 and 3.2 illustrate the impact of positively energizing leaders on both business unit and individual employee performance. These studies reveal that not only do positively energizing leaders affect business unit and employee performance, but their influence extends to the family life of employees as well. Employees' families are significantly influenced for the better by positive leaders (Owens, Baker, & Cameron, 2011).

(In Figure 3.1, the designation $p < .001$ indicates that the probability that this relationship occurs by chance is less than 1 in 1,000. That is, the relationship between the two factors is highly statistically significant.)

Leaders affect interpersonal relationships in their organizations by facilitating positive energy—both by modeling positive energy themselves and by diagnosing and

FIGURE 3.1   Impact of Positively Energizing Leaders on Employee Performance

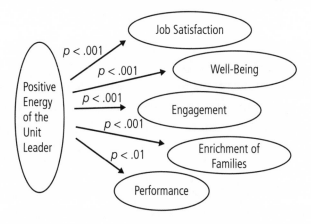

(SOURCE: Owens, Baker, & Cameron, 2011)

FIGURE 3.2 Impact of Positively Energizing Leaders on Unit Performance

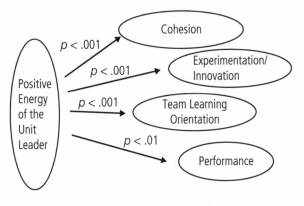

(SOURCE: Owens, Baker, & Cameron, 2011)

building positive-energy networks among others. Because interacting with a positive energizer is attractive (Baker & Dutton, 2007), positive relationships are more frequently formed. Leaders may not only radiate positive energy themselves, but they can identify the positive energizers with whom they work and recognize, reward, and support them. Because positive energizers affect the performance of others, positive energizers can be placed in tasks and roles that allow others to interact with them, for example, thus enhancing the performance of a broadened field of employees. They can be asked to coach or mentor others, and they can be selected to lead organizational change initiatives.

On the other hand, leaders often encounter individuals who are critical, cynical, and constantly disparaging, and who act as "black holes," destroying the good feelings and positive energy in others around them. How do positive leaders manage negative energizers, especially those who are essential to the organization for reasons of talent or experience (e.g., a highly skilled specialist who, nevertheless, serves as a "black hole" in the organization)? These people may best be approached using four sequential steps.

The first step is to provide direct, honest, and supportive feedback regarding the negative behaviors being demonstrated and the effects they are having on the organization. Most people will respond to authentic feedback that is meant to be helpful to them and to the organization. When people believe that someone cares, that someone will listen, and that there is an acceptable alternative available, the feedback they receive is usually sufficient to change behavior (Cameron, 2011).

If this step is ineffective, a second step is to provide development for the person. Often, negative energizers simply are unaware of substitute behavioral and emotional alternatives. They know no other way to respond. Coaching, mentoring, and training often prove effective in broadening the behavioral or response repertoire.

Third, if development does not work, place the individual in a noncentral position or role that minimizes the energy-depleting effects on others. This implies making the person peripheral or removing the opportunity for the negative energizer to have a negative impact on others. Provide an opportunity or a place for the person to succeed individually without affecting others in a negative way.

If none of these steps work—and this is a rare occurrence—the person may need to be given a chance to flourish elsewhere. Flourishing elsewhere means just that—helping the individual find a place where he or she can succeed. It does not mean merely firing someone and abandoning personal concern. Since neither the person nor the organization is flourishing in the current situation, help the person find another alternative. This fourth alternative should not be the first one selected, of course, but it should follow feedback and coaching on how to add positive energy to the system.

Not everyone is a positive energizer for everyone else, of course, and an individual may positively energize certain people but not others. Hence, conducting a diagnosis of the positive-energy network in an organization helps identify positive-energy hubs, black holes, and peripheral members who may need development.

This diagnosis can be done in a comprehensive and rigorous way by formal network analysis (Baker, 2000). This is accomplished by having all employees in a unit rate all the other employees on a one-to-seven scale with one representing "very de-energizing" and seven representing "very energizing." The data are submitted to a statistical program that produces a network map—similar to an airline magazine route map—showing the positive- and negative-energy connections in the organization. The map identifies those who positively energize the most people ("hubs" in the map), those who tend to de-energize people, and those on the periphery.

A more simplistic, but still useful, diagnosis is to ask employees to write down the names of the two, three, or four most energizing people in their organization. The results are tabulated so that the most frequently named individuals are identified—the positive energizers—as well as the names of individuals mentioned less frequently who can be mentored and developed. Positive energizers, for example, may be assigned to coach less energizing people. Task forces containing both high energizers and those with less positive energy could be formed to enhance and increase the positive energy of the group. And, recognition can be provided to positive energizers for the contributions their energy provides. Figure 3.3 provides an example of this simplified version of an energy map.

FIGURE 3.3 A Simplified Positive-Energy Network Map

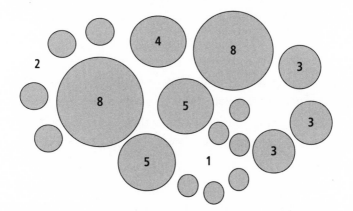

(Numbers indicate number of times mentioned as a positive energizer.)

Strengths

A second opportunity for leaders to promote positive relationships lies in reinforcing individual and organizational strengths. Identifying and building on people's strengths can produce greater benefit than finding and correcting their weaknesses (Buckingham & Clifton, 2001; Clifton & Harter, 2003; Seligman, 2002). For example, studies have shown that managers who spent more time with their strongest performers, as compared to spending it with their weakest performers, achieved double the productivity in their units. In organizations where workers have a chance each day to do what they do best or to demonstrate their strengths, productivity is one and a half times greater than in the typical organization (Clifton & Harter, 2003).

One reason for this difference in performance lies in the way that people learn. Individuals learn more readily and more completely from positive demonstrations than from negative demonstrations (Bruner & Goodnow, 1956). In other words, telling people what not to do is less helpful than identifying what they should do. People given negative examples (i.e., told what to fix or to avoid repeating) are much more likely to do exactly what they were told not to do, simply because that is the picture in their minds.

For example, if someone says to you, "Do not think of a white bear," the first thing you think of is a white bear, a phenomenon called the "ideomotor reflex" (Bargh & Chartrand, 1999). That is, thinking of an action makes people much more likely to engage in that action, regardless of whether or not they were thinking about doing it beforehand. Consequently, leaders who want to foster positive relationships emphasize strengths, small victories, and positive imagery with organization members as opposed to errors, mistakes, or problematic behaviors.

To illustrate this point, what if you were given a choice to either change or die? What if a well-informed authority figure told you that you had to make difficult and enduring changes in your behavior, and if you did not, your life would end soon? Would you change if it really mattered? What is the probability that people really change in these conditions?

The answer is that only one in nine people change. In studies of coronary artery bypass surgery patients who were living unhealthy lifestyles, almost 90 percent chose not to change their lifestyles after two years, even when threatened with death. However, when people were given a positive target for change (for example, we want to help you witness your daughter's wedding next summer, rather than "change or die"), 60 percent changed (Deutschman, 2005). Moving toward a positive target (or a strength) is much more effective than moving away from a negative target (or a weakness).

The impact of leaders who reinforce strengths among those with whom they work can be illustrated by a study of the performance of bowlers. In an experimental condition, people were videotaped as they bowled three games. Half of the bowlers were then shown videotapes of their spares or strikes, whereas the other half of the bowlers were shown videotapes of frames when they did not knock down all the pins. After a period of practice, using the videotapes as sources of feedback for change, statistically significant differences were found between the two groups. Those who watched themselves succeed (i.e., making strikes or spares) had improved significantly more than those who watched themselves in a nonsuccess condition (Kirschenbaum, 1984). That is, people tend to learn from and model positive imagery more effectively and efficiently than they follow negative imagery.

Leaders who enable positive deviance, therefore, emphasize successes, build on strengths, and celebrate the positive much more than spending time correcting the negative. They begin interactions and meetings with a celebration of what is going right. They role-model positive energy. They provide opportunities for other positive energizers to infuse members with their enthusiasm. They highlight positive images more than problematic images. Simply stated, they focus on strengths and encourage others to do so as well, thereby enabling the development of positive relationships.

An example of the effectiveness of positive relationships in achieving extraordinary success is illustrated by a quotation from a leader at the Rocky Flats Nuclear Arsenal three years before the project was completed (Cameron & Lavine, 2006: 165, 170, 181):

> It took years to change the attitude of the workforce. We got workers on board by listening to them, and unleashing their energy to do good work. The climate changed to one of working together. . . . That was the shift that really allowed us to make progress. It isn't much more magical than people sitting down together and actually solving problems together. . . . I said the very first day

I arrived at Rocky Flats: "This is the best team I've ever worked with," and I say that today. It is the best team I've ever worked with. . . . I think we have the best in the industry right now.

SUMMARY

The importance of enabling positive relationships in organizations is not news, but the impact of such relationships on multiple factors—including people's emotional and physiological health, life expectancy, and positively deviant performance in teams and organizations—is often unrecognized and worth reinforcing. Relationships that help people contribute to the benefit of others, rather than merely receive support from them, are the most valuable. Fostering positive energy in the organization and effectively managing positive energizers are also important elements in enabling these kinds of relationships. Helping individuals and organizations to become aware of and capitalize on their strengths has also been found to predict positive deviant performance.

ASSESSING POSITIVE LEADERSHIP ACTIVITIES

As a quick assessment of practical leadership activities that enable positive relationships, the following diagnostic questions may be helpful. Use the following scale to respond.

1 — Never 2 — Seldom 3 — Sometimes
4 — Frequently 5 — Always

As a leader, to what extent do you:

_____ Ensure that employees have an opportunity to provide emotional, intellectual, or physical support *to* others in addition to receiving support *from* the organization?

_____ Model positive energy yourself, and also recognize and encourage other positive energizers in your organization?

_____ Diagnose your organization's energy networks, so that you support and utilize individuals in energy hubs as well as help develop peripheral members?

_____ Provide more feedback to individuals on their strengths rather than on their weaknesses?

_____ Spend more time with your strongest performers than with your weakest performers?

_____ Establish positive targets rather than focusing on solving problems or getting rid of obstacles?

CHAPTER

4

Positive
Communication

Positive communication occurs in organizations when affirmative and supportive language replaces negative and critical language. The power of positive communication is illustrated in a study of 60 top-management teams, who were engaged in annual strategic-planning, problem-solving, and budget-setting activities (Losada & Heaphy, 2004) that investigated why some management teams performed better than others.

Teams of senior managers who worked together on a regular basis were categorized as high, medium, or low performing based on three measures of performance in their organizations: productivity, customer satisfaction, and 360-degree evaluations of the managers' competency comprising the teams. Combining these criteria in the

60 teams, 15 were rated as high, 26 as medium, and 19 as low in their performance.

To explain differences among the teams, the communication patterns of team members were carefully monitored during the workday and categorized by trained raters who were unaware of the performance level of the teams. Four communication categories were used: the ratio of *positive* to *negative* comments, the ratio of *inquiry* to *advocacy* comments, the ratio of a focus on *others* compared to a focus on *self*, and a measure of *connectivity*, or the amount of interaction, engagement, and information exchanged in the team.

The single most important factor in predicting organizational performance—which was more than twice as powerful as any other factor—was the ratio of positive statements to negative statements. Positive statements are those that express appreciation, support, helpfulness, approval, or compliments. Negative statements express criticism, disapproval, dissatisfaction, cynicism, or disagreement.

As shown in Table 4.1, the results of the research revealed that in high-performing organizations, the ratio of positive to negative statements in their top-management teams was 5.6 to 1. Five times more positive statements were made than negative statements as high-performing teams engaged in work. In medium-performing organizations, the ratio was 1.8 to 1. In low-performing organizations, the ratio was 0.36 to 1. In organizations that performed poorly, in other words, three times as many negative comments were made as positive comments among top-management members. (This study, by the way, utilized

TABLE 4.1 Communication in Top-Management Teams	TEAM PERFORMANCE		
	High	Medium	Low
Positive Statement Ratio	5.6 to 1	1.8 to 1	0.36 to 1
(supportive, encouraging, appreciation versus critical, disapproval, contradictory)			
Inquiry/Advocacy Ratio	1.1 to 1	0.67 to 1	0.05 to 1
(questioning versus asserting)			
Others/Self Ratio	0.94 to 1	0.62 to 1	0.03 to 1
(external versus internal focus)			
Connectivity Average	32	22	18
(mutual influence, assistance, interaction)			
Source: Losada & Heaphy, 2004			

nonlinear dynamics and Lorenz attractor diagrams, so causal directionality could be projected. Results were not merely a product of positive talk resulting from high performance.)

Other dimensions of communication were also important in differentiating high-performing from low-performing organizations. For example, team members in high-performing organizations were found to be essentially balanced in the number of *inquiry* statements (i.e., asking questions, seeking others' viewpoints) compared to *advocacy* statements (i.e., telling, or advocating a position), whereas low-performing organizations were highly overloaded toward advocacy rather than inquiry. High performers had a ratio of 1.1 inquiries for every 1.0 advocacy statement. Low performers had a ratio of 0.05 to 1, or 5 inquiries for every 100 advocacy statements.

A relative balance also existed in the focus on *self* versus *others* in high-performing organizations (0.94 statements focused on others for every 1.0 statement focused on self), whereas low-performing organizations were heavily overloaded in their focus on self (3 statements focused on others' perspectives for every 100 statements focused on self).

Finally, in measures of connectivity (engagement, information flows, participation), the ratio was almost twice as high for high-performing organizations as for low-performing organizations (32 compared to 18). Moreover, the correlation between the positive-to-negative statement ratio and connectivity—or the engagement of team members—was 0.9. Positive communication predicted employee engagement.

These results demonstrate that high-performing organizations had different communication patterns than low-performing organizations—primarily based on the abundance of positive comments among top-management team members. Highly effective organizations were far more complimentary and supportive than low-performing organizations. It is not that correction and criticism were entirely absent; that is, these organizations were not characterized by a Pollyannaish or rose-colored-glasses approach to work. The ratio, it is important to point out, was not 5 to

0, or 20 to 1. Correction, criticism, and confrontation were present, but they were offered in a positive context.

As discovered by Fredrickson and Losada (2005), a ratio of between 3 and approximately 8 positive statements to every 1 negative statement is predictive of the highest levels of performance. Negative communications were present in high-performing organizations but just not to the extent that they dominated or even matched the positive. Organizations that performed moderately well had about an equal number of positive and negative comments, and organizations that performed poorly were more negative than positive (Losada & Heaphy, 2004).

This same 5 to 1 ratio was discovered by Gottman (1994) in his predictive studies of successful marriages and divorces. In a study where couples were recorded for 15 minutes as they conversed about a topic that was controversial in their relationships (e.g., child rearing, budget, time at work), the best predictor of the sustainability and quality of the marital relationship was the ratio of positive to negative communication events. The "Gottman index," in fact, has made the 5 to 1 ratio quite well accepted in family therapy and family sociology based on the finding that marriages that end in divorce and marriages that are judged to be unhappy and unfulfilling are typified by more negative than positive communication interactions (Gottman, 1994). After following these couples for ten years, Gottman could predict with a high degree of accuracy which couples were still married and were happily married, based on the 15-minute conversation a decade earlier. The predictive ratio was the same 5 to 1 ratio of positive to negative state-ments.

A similar finding is associated with experienced emo-tions and performance. Because positive comments tend to engender positive emotions, Fredrickson and Losada (2005) studied the relationships between emotions and performance. They found evidence from several psycho-logical studies that people who experience a ratio of at least three positive emotions for every negative emotion tend to flourish in mental health and individual perfor-mance (Fredrickson & Losada, 2005). Table 4.2 summa-rizes the results of a variety of studies showing the positive outcomes associated with a 3 to 1 ratio or higher of posi-tive to negative emotions (Diener & Biswas-Diener, 2008; Fredrickson, 2009).

Another effect of positive communication is illustrated by an oft-replicated study of ninth-grade students enrolled in literature classes. A substantial portion of the classical literature in the Western world is tragedy, or negatively oriented literature. In these experiments, half the stu-dents were exposed to positive, virtuous communication—including practicing virtuous behaviors—and the other half served as the control group. Students were assigned, for example, to do a kind deed each day during a specific week and then to write about it or discuss it with others.

Figure 4.1 summarizes the results. Students exposed to positive and virtuous communication—including talk-ing and writing about their virtuous practices during the semester—were significantly advantaged regarding out-comes such as zest for learning, social skills, writing com-

TABLE 4.2 The Effects of at Least a 3 to 1 Positivity Ratio
• People live longer (+11 years).
• People succumb to fewer illnesses.
• People have higher survival rates after a serious illness or an accident.
• People stay married longer.
• People tolerate pain better.
• People work harder.
• People perform better on the job.
• People make more money (+30 percent).
• People display more mental acuity.
• People make higher-quality decisions.
• People are more creative and more flexible in their thinking.
• People are more adaptive and resilient after trials and trauma.
• People engage in more helping behaviors and citizenship activities.

petence, absence of depression, and course grades compared to the control groups.

One explanation for the performance effects of positive communication is that positive communication has been found to create significantly more "connectivity"—that is, the exchange of information, interpersonal interactions, and positive emotions—in organizations. This connectivity is the means by which resources flow and coordinated action takes place (Losada & Heaphy, 2004). Coordinated exchange, in turn, enables higher productivity and higher-quality performance because it facilitates the formation of

FIGURE 4.1   A Comparison of Ninth-Grade Literature
Class Students' Performances

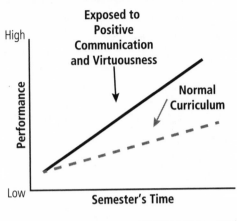

(SOURCE: Seligman, 2011)

needed social capital and synchronicity (Dutton & Heaphy,
2003; Fredrickson & Losada, 2005; Fredrickson, Mancuso,
Branigan, & Tugade, 2000; Losada, 1999).

ENABLING POSITIVE COMMUNICATION

Because most people react more strongly to bad than to
good (Baumeister et al., 2001), and because most organizations are fraught with problems and challenges, prescrib-
ing positive communication is much easier than practicing
it. One obvious way that leaders enable positive communication is by using positive talk themselves. Minimizing
criticism and negativity, and replacing them with an abundance of positive feedback and expressions of support, can

enable the affirmative effects of communication. Because leaders' role modeling has an exponential effect on creating such outcomes in organizations (George, 1998), the communication patterns of leaders are especially important.

Communicating authentically and communicating sincerely are requisite characteristics of such positive talk by leaders, of course, because comments that appear to be untrustworthy or disingenuous have the reverse effect. Moreover, the appropriate positive-to-negative statement ratio is crucial for maintaining balance and motivation. Too much positivity can foster complacency and mediocrity, and too much negativity can lead to defensiveness and withdrawal (Cameron, 2011).

In addition to role modeling, two specific strategies are available for facilitating positive communication in organizations: *the reflected best-self feedback* process (Roberts, et al., 2004) and the use of *supportive communication* (Cameron, 2011).

Best-self feedback

When people receive feedback from others—as in 360 feedback reports—the tendency is to focus on the lowest scores or the negative information. Most of the time, people target improvement in their weaknesses as their priority. The reflected best-self feedback process, on the other hand, is based on the impact of positive feedback on individual improvement. It is a technique used to capture information that uncovers and highlights an individual's talents and highest capabilities. It encourages positive communication and then guides people through a process of uncovering their strengths and the positive attributes that are perceived by others. The technique was developed at the University of Michigan and is now being used in a variety of universities and corporations (Roberts et al., 2004).

The process works as follows. An individual identifies approximately 20 acquaintances. These can be friends, coworkers, neighbors, family members, or representatives from all these groups. Each of these acquaintances is asked to write three short anecdotes in response to the question "When you have seen me make a special or important contribution, what distinctive strengths did I display?" Or, alternatively, "When you have seen me at my best, what unique value did I create?"

In other words, the 20 acquaintances write three anecdotes about a time when this person displayed her or his best self. The 60 anecdotes identify the key behavioral strengths and unique talents of the individual—information that is both rare and extremely valuable. This communication is designed to be universally positive and to uncover strengths and abilities that individuals often cannot identify themselves, and the concomitant positive effects of positive feedback naturally follow (Roberts et al., 2004).

This positive information is analyzed by the person who receives the stories. He or she summarizes the key themes and develops a best-self portrait. These themes represent the best-self strengths and unique contributions of the person, and the person can be assisted in identifying strategies for capitalizing on these strengths. A process for developing such strategies is available at www.bus.umich.edu/positive (*Reflected Best-Self Exercise Suite of Products*).

The feedback comes in the form of retold incidents and stories, not numbers or trend lines, so it is connected directly to behaviors that the person has displayed in the past and that can be repeated and enhanced in the future. The stories capture emotions and feelings as well as intentional actions, so the feedback provides a rich array of information for individuals to analyze. Almost always, strengths and abilities that people would never mark on a "strengths finder" checklist (Buckingham & Clifton, 2001) are uncovered because such strengths are so natural and easily displayed that people take these strengths for granted. People often discover that they add unique value in circumstances that are natural and almost effortless in their interactions.

The result of this feedback is a personal agenda for capitalizing on and expanding positive attributes that are not necessarily conscious or obvious to the individual. Providing feedback on weaknesses and deficiencies is also important, of course, but a focus on weaknesses or deficiencies will lead only to the development of competence (Clifton & Harter, 2003), whereas a focus on strengths can lead to excellence and positively deviant performance.

Additional benefits of best-self feedback are that feedback recipients often have strengthened relationships with feedback givers, a desire for reciprocity grows, an enhanced desire to live up to the positive best-self descriptions emerges, and a reinterpretation of past personal history as being more strength-based occurs. When best-self feedback is practiced in organizations, cohesion and mutual support are positively affected (Roberts et al., 2004).

Of course, completely ignoring weaknesses and inadequacies is not healthy and focusing exclusively on the positive—while disregarding critical deficiencies—is not apt to be productive in the long run. As has been pointed out, however, most individuals, as well as most organizations, concentrate overwhelmingly on the negative, and they are likely to ignore, or at least give short shrift to, positive feedback. The reflected best-self feedback process is a way to counterbalance this tendency by encouraging and enabling positive communication. It strengthens relationships between feedback providers and receivers, it fosters positive interactions and reciprocal feedback, it enhances feelings of closeness among individuals, and it provides the positive energy needed to embark on personal improvement efforts.

Leaders may not have the wherewithal to implement a complete best-self feedback process across their organizations, but they can provide regular feedback to others that highlights valuable contributions, unique strengths, and displays of positive qualities on an ongoing basis. In addition, a variation on the best-self feedback process can be implemented in a small group or a team. Each person in the group is provided a set of 5×7 cards—one for each other person in the group. On one side of the card, the person writes a response to these statements: "Here is what I especially value about your contribution to our team." "Here are the special strengths you display." "Here is what I admire about you." On the reverse side of the card, the person writes a response to these statements: "If we are to exceed our aspirations, if we are to become extraordinary, if we are to be the benchmark that others try to emulate, here is what we need you to do." "Here is how we need you to create additional value." Each group member receives a card from each of the other members of the team, analyzes the feedback, and then publicly verbalizes the strengths others value as well as the additional contributions that can be made in pursuit of positive deviance. This feedback, similar to the reflected best-self feedback, is focused exclusively on strengths and contributions, not on weaknesses or limitations.

Supportive communication

The use of *supportive communication* is another means by which leaders can enable positive deviance through their feedback, particularly when corrective, critical, or negative messages must be delivered (Cameron, 2011). All communication cannot be complimentary, agreeable, or focused on the best self, of course, and negative messages must always be delivered at some point. Mistakes are made, corrections are required, and disapproving statements are necessary and healthy in any relationship.

It is not difficult to communicate positively—to express confidence, trust, and openness—when things are going well and when people are doing what they should be doing. But when someone else's behavior must be corrected, when negative feedback must be provided, or when the shortcomings of another person must be pointed out, communicating in a way that builds and strengthens the relationship is more difficult.

This type of communication is called supportive communication because it seeks to preserve, support, and enhance a positive relationship while still addressing a problematic or an uncomfortable issue, giving negative feedback, or communicating uncomplimentary information (Gibb, 1961; Knapp & Vangelisti, 1996). A great deal of evidence confirms that supportive communication is a prerequisite for and enabler of especially positive organizational performance (Dutton, 2003; Spitzberg, 1994).

Supportive communication consists of at least eight communication strategies: congruent, problem-centered, validating, conjunctive, specific, owned, reflective listening, and descriptive (see Cameron, 2011, for a discussion of each of these strategies).

One of the most important and powerful of these techniques is the use of *descriptive statements* rather than *evaluative statements* in identifying and resolving problems (Rogers, 1961). Here is the difference between the two.

Evaluative communication makes a judgment or places a label on other individuals or on their behavior (e.g., "You are wrong," "You are incompetent," "This is your fault"). These kinds of statements generally make recipients feel attacked and, consequently, they respond defensively, feel devalued and worthless, and withdraw or quit trying. The frequency and accuracy of subsequent communication and the quality of the relationship deteriorate (Rogers, 1961). Evaluative statements are usually made because people do not know how to be honest and authentic without being judgmental or evaluative of another person when things go wrong.

To illustrate, the following interaction occurred in a firm—B.A.S.—in response to a presentation by a marketing manager. He was assigned to introduce a new goal-setting program as a way to address some productivity problems in the company. After his carefully prepared presentation in the management meeting, one of the senior executives responded: "In my opinion, this is a naive approach to solving our productivity issues. The considerations are much more complex than this guy seems to realize. I don't think we should waste our time by pursuing this plan any further."

The senior executive's opinion may be justified, but the manner in which he delivered the message probably eliminated any hope of its being dealt with objectively. Certainly, the marketing manager's motivation to creatively respond was diminished as he felt personally attacked and denigrated.

An alternative to evaluation is *descriptive communication*, which allows a person to be authentic and helpful when providing negative information. Descriptive communication involves three steps. First, provide an objective description of the event that occurred or the behavior that needs to be modified. Deliver this objective description as dispassionately as possible and focus on the action or event, not the person. The description should identify elements of the behavior that can be confirmed by objective observers (they are valid), that are under the control of the recipient (they are changeable), and that can be compared to accepted standards rather than to personal opinions or preferences (they are factual). Subjective impressions or attributions to the motives of another person are avoided.

Second, describe reactions to or consequences of the behavior. Rather than projecting onto another person the cause of the problem or the supposed rationale for the behavior, focus on the reactions or consequences the behavior produced. This requires communicators to be aware of their own feelings and reactions and able to describe them. Using one-word descriptions for feelings is often the best method: "I'm concerned about our productivity," "Your level of accomplishment frustrates me," or "This makes me uncomfortable." Similarly, point out the consequences of the behavior: "Profits are off this month," "Department quality ratings are down," or "Two customers have called in to express dissatisfaction."

Describing feelings or consequences also lessens the likelihood of defensiveness, since the problem is framed in the context of the communicator's feelings or objective consequences, not the personal attributes of the other person. If those feelings or consequences are described in a nonaccusing way, the major energies of the communicators can be focused on problem solving rather than on defending against evaluations or perceived attacks.

The third step is to suggest a more acceptable alternative. This focuses the discussion on possible solutions to the problem, not on the person. It also helps the individual save face and avoid feeling personally criticized because she or he is separated from the behavior. Self-esteem is preserved because it is a controllable behavior, not the person or the personality, that should be modified. The emphasis is on finding a solution that is acceptable to both parties, not on deciding who is right and who is wrong or who should change and who should not. Consequently, the relationship is preserved and even strengthened by communicating a message of support.

In the case of the marketing manager's goal-setting proposal in B.A.S., a more positive alternative might be for the senior executive to reply: "This is an interesting proposal, and I appreciate your thoughtfulness in developing it. I see some issues that are not addressed by what you have proposed [*description*], and I am not comfortable approving the proposal as it has been presented [*feelings*]. I suggest that we create a small task force to assist you in addressing some of the unresolved issues [*suggestion*]." The likelihood of productive follow-up action is markedly greater with this kind of reply.

In sum, when delivering negative messages, three steps are necessary:

(1)   Describe a situation (rather than evaluate it).

(2)   Identify objective consequences or personal feelings associated with it (rather than place blame).

(3)   Suggest acceptable alternatives (rather than argue about who is right or at fault).

Implementing these three steps leads to a constructive conversation that emphasizes commonalities and collaborating rather than arguing or judging (Rogers & Farson, 1976). It provides support for the recipient while still delivering negative messages. Any lingering disagreements focus on determining which alternative is most acceptable rather than defending, arguing, or proving who is at fault.

Other strategies of supportive communication include maintaining *congruence* among the words, thoughts, and feelings of the communicator (i.e., being authentic and sincere); remaining *problem-focused* rather than person-focused (i.e., concentrating on the action, not on the person); using *validation* (i.e., communicating that the person's perspective has merit); being *specific* (i.e., referring to an actual example or behavior) and using *conjunctive* statements (i.e., connecting directly to the preceding message or to the person's response); personally *owning* the communication (i.e., taking personal responsibility for the message); and demonstrating *active listening* and appropriate *response types* (i.e., using reflective, probing, deflecting, and advising responses appropriately) (for a thorough description of these attributes, see Cameron, 2011).

SUMMARY

To enable positive communication in organizations, consciously pay attention to the positivity ratio, so that more positive than negative messages are delivered. Provide feedback on strengths, unique contributions, and best-self demonstrations. Use supportive strategies—especially when critical or corrective messages must be delivered. The communication patterns of leaders are a powerful factor in enabling positively deviant performance to emerge. Therefore, because both positive and negative messages need to be delivered, they should be delivered in supportive, growth-producing ways.

ASSESSING POSITIVE LEADERSHIP ACTIVITIES

As a quick assessment of practical leadership activities that enable positive communication, the following diagnostic questions may be helpful. Use the following scale to respond.

---

1 — Never 2 — Seldom 3 — Sometimes
4 — Frequently 5 — Always

As a leader, to what extent do you:

_____ Communicate a ratio of approximately five positive messages for every negative message to those with whom you interact?

_____ Provide opportunities for employees to receive best-self feedback and develop best-self portraits?

_____ Consistently distribute notes or cards to your employees complimenting their performance?

_____ Provide negative feedback in supportive ways— especially using descriptive rather than evaluative statements—so that the relationship is strengthened?

_____ Focus on the detrimental _behavior_ and its consequences, not on the person, when correcting people or providing negative feedback?

CHAPTER

5

Positive
Meaning

The search for positive meaning has been proposed as a universal human need (Baumeister & Vohs, 2002; Frankl, 1959; Grant, 2007), and well-established relationships exist between engaging in meaningful work and positive outcomes. When people feel that they are pursuing a profound purpose or engaging in work that is personally important, significant positive effects are produced, including reductions in stress, depression, turnover, absenteeism, dissatisfaction, and cynicism, as well as increases in commitment, effort, engagement, empowerment, happiness, satisfaction, and a sense of fulfillment (see Chen, 2007).

Wrzesniewski (2003), citing research in sociology (Bellah, et al., 1985) and psychology (Baumeister, 1991; Schwartz,

1994), pointed out that individuals typically associate one of three kinds of meaning with work. They define their work as a *job*, as a *career*, or as a *calling*.

Those who see work as a *job* do their work primarily for the financial or material rewards it provides. They gain no particular personal satisfaction from the work, and they pursue their interests and passions in nonwork settings. Work is a means for obtaining financial or other resources to engage in some other activity (e.g., "Give me the assignment, and I'll do it. This job helps me make my car payments").

In contrast, individuals with a *career* orientation are motivated by accomplishment and success. They work to achieve the prestige, power, recognition, and advancement that come from performing their work well. They desire to be distinguished members of their organizations, and they use work to acquire promotion, notoriety, title, or advancement. Work is a means for achieving personal growth, recognition, and capability development (e.g., "I want to reach a senior leadership position in this organization").

The third orientation, the sense of work as a *calling*, characterizes individuals who are driven by the meaning associated with the work itself. The actual tasks involved in their work provide intrinsic motivation and profound purpose. They consider work inherently fulfilling, and they seek for a greater good, regardless of the material rewards offered by the work. Their work possesses a sense of meaning that reaches beyond personal benefit or the acquisition of reward (e.g., "I care deeply about what I am doing at work").

Paralleling these work orientations are three types of relationships between members and their organizations: *compliance, identification,* and *internalization* (Kelman, 1958; O'Reilly & Chatman, 1996). These researchers identified different types of connections that people develop with their employing organization, and these connections are similar to Wrzesniewski's (2003) orientations toward the meaning of work.

A *compliance* relationship produces desired behaviors through punishments and rewards. That is, compliant individuals act for personal material benefit and do not necessarily believe in the content of the action they take (i.e., a *job* orientation). They conform to organizational rules and procedures and produce results not because of an inherent drive but because the reward and punishment system demands it. Their behavior complies with what the organization expects.

Individuals with an *identification* relationship are motivated to maintain a more engaged relationship with the organization. These individuals are committed to what they do as organizational members, and they seek involvement and contribution. They work to procure the satisfaction of belonging and to reinforce a sense of membership (i.e., a *career* orientation). The relationship produces mutual benefits to both the employee and the organization.

Internalization is a relationship defined by a complete and absolute adoption of organizational goals. Individuals who have internalized the organizational culture and mission have a conviction that what they are doing is right and good. Internalization leads individuals to adopt the organization's purposes and priorities as their own (i.e., a *calling* orientation). Their loyalty to the organization is unequivocal, and their behavior embodies the values, mission, and activities to which the organization subscribes.

These orientations toward a sense of calling and internalization in work are associated with the concept of *meaningfulness*. The more that individuals define their work as a calling and have a conviction that what they are doing is good and right, the more meaningful the work (Grant, 2008). High levels of meaningfulness in work have been found to be associated with positive outcomes and extraordinary individual and organizational performance.

For example, workers with a calling orientation reported higher job and life satisfaction scores compared to those with career or job orientations. They also experienced higher satisfaction with their organization and with their work (Wrzesniewski, McCauley, Rozin, & Schwartz, 1997). A stronger identification with the work unit accompanied a calling orientation, as did higher levels of trust and confidence in management, higher levels of commitment to the organization, less conflict, more satisfactory relationships with coworkers, and higher levels of satisfaction with the tasks themselves (Cook & Wall, 1980; Mowday, Steers, & Porter, 1979; Taylor & Bowers, 1972).

These high satisfaction scores are likely to be associated with higher performance—based on Judge, Thoreson, Bono, and Patton's (2001) definitive meta-analysis, which shows that the average correlation between job satisfaction and performance is 0.30—and the relationship between a sense of calling and satisfaction is significant (Wrzesniewski, 2003). In fact, significantly higher levels of organizational performance were detected in health-care organizations when a sense of calling predominated among employees (Wrzesniewski & Dutton, in press; Wrzesniewski & Landman, 2000).

In especially enlightening studies of the effects of meaningfulness in work, Grant et al. (2007, 2008) conducted investigations of telephone solicitors (mostly students working in part-time jobs). The task of these students was to place calls to university alumni requesting donations. The trouble was, these callers experienced almost universal rejection from the recipients of their calls. Little motivation to produce was associated with the job inasmuch as the callers were required to read a standardized script, and they received little information about the success or impact of their work. The voluntary turnover rate among the callers was approximately 350 percent.

In the study, half of the callers were exposed for just five minutes to a scholarship student who benefited from the solicitations. This student simply thanked the callers for their efforts and explained to them the meaningfulness of the work they were doing. The scholarship student communicated, for example, that he or she would not have been able to attend the university had these solicitors not raised the money that provided the scholarship funds. The other half of the callers were not exposed to a scholarship student and received no such message.

Figures 5.1 through 5.4 summarize the results of the studies (Grant, 2007, 2008; Grant et al., 2007). It is easy to see the impact of having a sense of the meaningfulness

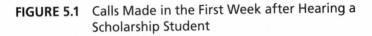

FIGURE 5.1 Calls Made in the First Week after Hearing a Scholarship Student

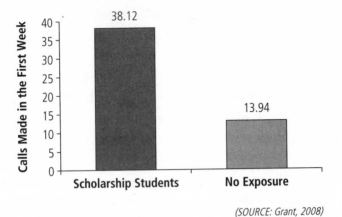

(SOURCE: Grant, 2008)

FIGURE 5.2 Pledges Obtained in the First Week

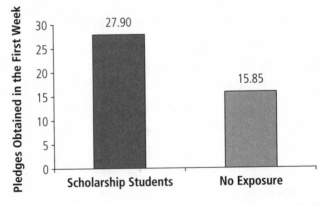

(SOURCE: Grant, 2008)

FIGURE 5.3 Minutes on the Phone per Week after One Month

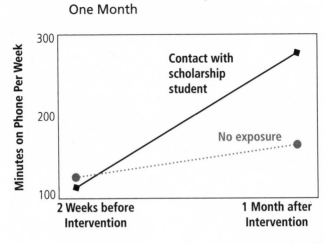

(SOURCE: Grant et al., 2007)

FIGURE 5.4 Amount of Pledges Obtained

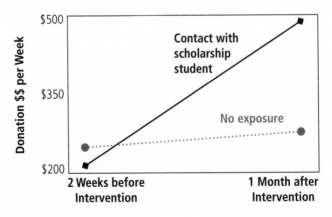

(SOURCE: Grant et al., 2007)

associated with work. Callers exposed to a scholarship student increased their effort, productivity, and effectiveness in successfully accomplishing the job by almost a factor of three compared to callers who received no information about meaningfulness. The results not only were seen immediately after the intervention (a week later) but the consequences could be seen at least a month later!

It is important to remember that a sense of calling is not dependent on the type of work performed; rather, it is associated with the positive meaning inherent in the work (Bellah et al., 1985; Wrzesniewski, 2003). Any kind of work—even that typically thought of as physically, socially, or morally tainted—can be reframed in a positive light (Ashforth & Kreiner, 1999). Put another way, exactly the same task may be viewed as a job or a calling depending on the perspective of the individual.

For example, in a study of custodians who worked in a hospital in the Midwest (Wrzesniewski & Dutton, in press), researchers interviewed a staff member who was assigned to clean up vomit and excrement in the oncology ward when patients came in for chemotherapy. These patients sometimes lost control of bodily functions when they were subjected to medications needed to treat their malignancies. They were often at their very worst in these conditions—physically ill, emotionally embarrassed, and fearful of the outcomes.

A staff member's response to her work was characterized by the following statement: "My job is equally important to the physician. I help these people feel human.

At their lowest and most vulnerable point, I help them maintain their dignity. I make it okay to feel awful, to lose control, and to be unable to manage themselves. My role is crucial to the healing process." Even the most noxious and unpleasant of tasks can be reinterpreted as a calling that has a profound purpose (Pratt & Ashforth, 2003).

ENABLING POSITIVE MEANING

Early management theorists (Barnard, 1968; Selznick, 1984; Weber, 1992) believed that the primary responsibility of the leader was to infuse purpose and meaning into the work lives of organization members. Instead of merely focusing on economic performance, managing the production function, or positioning the organization for competitive advantage, meaning-making was seen by these writers as the primary function of an executive. Unfortunately, in subsequent decades less emphasis has been placed on the leader's role in clarifying and enhancing meaningfulness.

Work is associated with meaningfulness when it possesses one or more of four key attributes:

(1)   The work has an important positive impact on the well-being of human beings (Brown, Nesse, Vinokur, & Smith, 2003; Grant, 2008; Grant et al., 2007).

(2)   The work is associated with an important virtue or a personal value (Bright, Cameron, & Caza, 2006; Weber, 1992).

(3) The work has an impact that extends beyond the immediate time frame or creates a ripple effect (Cameron & Lavine, 2006; Crocker, Nuer, Olivier, & Cohen, 2006).

(4) The work builds supportive relationships or a sense of community in people (Polodny, Khurana, & Hill-Popper, 2005; Rousseau, 1992).

Regarding the first attribute, *positive impact on others*, studies of job design by Hackman and Oldham (1980) found that workers who could see the effects of their work on others—who were aware of the contributions they made to the welfare of people—had a significantly higher sense of meaningfulness, and their subsequent performance and engagement in the organization were significantly higher. Several studies have found that workers who were given direct contact with the beneficiaries of their work had significantly greater productivity in routine tasks, and they produced more than one-and-a-half times the output of those who did not have contact with beneficiaries (Grant et al., 2007).

Ensuring that individuals are given opportunities to interact directly with those receiving their output or service, and to receive feedback regarding the impact of what they do, has proven to be an effective leadership strategy for fostering a sense of meaningfulness in work. Some companies, for example, Medtronic, regularly invite patients whose lives have been transformed by the medical devices they manufacture to give speeches at employee gatherings. Google posts comments from customers, some of them indicating the life-changing benefits of using Google, on its company website. Huffy manufacturing employees visit customers to observe how people use their products and how these products affect their lifestyles.

The second attribute, *associating work with core individual values*, depends on highlighting the connections between what is most meaningful to individuals and the benefits produced by the organization. Of course, what people value may vary a great deal, but certain values tend to be nearly universal, for example, caring, helpfulness, frugality, and assisting the disadvantaged. Attaching the work to such values tends to enhance its meaningfulness for individuals.

For example, Mark Schwartz, CEO at Timberland, decided to substantially increase the percentage of organically grown cotton in the clothes the company manufactures in order to reduce exposure to carcinogens by migrant workers who pick corporately grown cotton. Even in the absence of any customer demand or regulatory encouragement, and at a substantial expense to the company's bottom line, Schwartz's intention was to provide a benefit to a disadvantaged group of individuals who would likely never be customers but whose lives could be made better by Timberland's change in policy (Schwartz, 2001). He stated:

> We make boots, shoes, shirts, jackets, and other apparel. That's what we do, but that's not who we are. We believe that doing good and doing well are not separable ideas. No consumer cares about the health of cotton pickers. People who buy our products don't care about the carcinogenic pesticides sprayed on cotton. But we care. We don't know all the solutions, but we're trying to work to find them.

Similarly, in an attempt to marry his theological and free-enterprise values, Tom Chappell, founder of Tom's of Maine, created products void of dyes, sweeteners, and preservatives two decades before it became the socially accepted thing to do for health-conscious companies. He also established a policy in his firm in which 10 percent of all profits and 5 percent of employees' time would be donated annually to charitable organizations. The motive was not public recognition or marketing advantage—since these decisions were made at a time when such moves were considered imprudent—but "just because it is the right thing to do" (Chappell, 1999).

Highlighting the connections between the organization's output and the values that employees care deeply about—in these cases, protecting the health of and providing benefit to disadvantaged populations as well as to the planet—exemplifies a second way to enable meaningfulness in and of work (Pratt & Ashforth, 2003).

The third attribute, *highlighting the long-term impact of the work*, also enhances its meaningfulness. According to a number of authors such as Lawrence and Nohria (2002) and Covey (2004), a basic human need or drive is to create a legacy, or to extend influence beyond the immediate time frame. Rather than to seek merely for immediate personal benefit or self-aggrandizement, these authors highlighted the performance benefits of having an effect on long-term consequences.

Cameron and Lavine (2006) documented this effect in studying the positively deviant performance of the cleanup of the Rocky Flats Nuclear Arsenal in a previously considered impossible time frame, budget, and cleanliness standard. Union members had to be willing to work themselves out of a job as quickly as possible—a stance completely contradictory to the fundamental purposes of unions—while maintaining high levels of morale and safety among remaining workers. This remarkable performance was dependent on highlighting the long-term effects on the successful accomplishment of the work. Employees found profound meaningfulness in what they believed to be a multigenerational impact of their efforts. The fact that a dangerous location would be removed but also that it would become a wildlife refuge—the only such site on the eastern slope of the Rocky Mountains, and a safe environment for a thousand years to come—was a driving force in motivating the sacrifices that were required to succeed.

Meaningfulness and long-term legacy are closely linked, as illustrated by Congressman Joe Knollenberg, a liaison to Congress for the Rocky Flats project:

> We call it "catch the fever" because you are actually becoming part of something historical. Most everyone now is proud of the work they do, even the steelworkers union, the trade unions, the guards union. They are proud of what they do, and they are proud to be able to achieve something special. Everyone wants meaning in their job. Now they are back to work and the buildings are going away. Building 771 was the most dangerous building in the world, and now it's not. It's going to come down shortly. We are proud of our achievements, and they are too. (Cameron & Lavine, 2006: 126–127)

Fourth, *building a sense of community* is another of the central premises of meaningfulness (Polodny, Khurana, & Hill-Popper, 2005). Some authors have claimed, in fact, that this attribute is the fundamental feature of meaningfulness (Rousseau, 1992). One especially noteworthy way for leaders to enable a sense of meaningfulness in community is to reinforce and sponsor *contribution goals*.

For example, Crocker and Park (2004) found that the goals individuals pursue can be categorized into two types. Most people pursue both kinds of goals, but one or the other type tends to predominate. One type of goal is an emphasis on self-interest or personal achievement. This goal focuses on obtaining a desired outcome or a preferred reward, accomplishing something that brings self-satisfaction, enhancing self-esteem, or creating a positive self-image in the eyes of others. Individuals who emphasize this type of goal are primarily interested in proving themselves, reinforcing their self-worth, or demonstrating their competency. Attaining desired performance outcomes is the primary objective.

The other type of goal focuses on providing a benefit to others or on making a contribution. This type of goal centers on what individuals can give compared to what they can get. A contribution goal is motivated more by benevolence than by a desire for acquisition. Crocker, Nuer, Olivier, and Cohen (2006) found that goals focused on contributing to others produced a *growth* orientation in individuals over time, whereas self-interest goals produced a *proving* orientation over time.

In studies of individuals over a five- or six-month period, Crocker and colleagues (2006) found that contribution goals led to significantly more learning and development, higher levels of interpersonal trust, more supportive relationships, and less depression and loneliness than did self-interest goals. Most importantly, when contribution goals predominated, the meaningfulness of activities was substantially higher than when self-interest goals predominated (Niiya & Crocker, 2008).

These findings are consistent with several other studies that also highlight the importance of contribution goals compared to self-interest goals. As mentioned earlier, Brown, Nesse, Vinokur, and Smith (2003) and Brown and Brown (2006) found that the contribution individuals make to a relationship, not what they receive from that relationship, is significant in accounting for meaningfulness and positive outcomes. In a study of patients on kidney dialysis machines, for example, measurements were taken of their emotional and physical health as well as the extent to which they were *receiving* love, support, and encouragement and *providing* love, support, and encouragement to others. Even though they were immobile and could not physically respond, patients enjoyed better health when they felt they were *contributing* to the well-being of others through support, love, and encouragement than when they were *receiving* these things. Contribution-focused goals produced significantly more mental, emotional, and physiological benefits than self-achievement-focused goals.

Similarly, in studies of the language that people use to describe their work experiences, Pennebaker (2002) found that a predominance of the word "we" was associated with more meaningfulness and engagement when applied to work than the predominance of the word "I." Positive meaning, in other words, was associated with contribution to and engagement with others significantly more than self-focused activity.

SUMMARY

Leaders who enable meaningfulness in work are interested in highlighting the value associated with the organization's outcomes, which extends beyond the personal benefit of individual employees. They are conscious of the different orientations that individuals possess regarding their work (job, career, or calling) and toward the organization itself (compliance, identification, or internalization). Since positively deviant performance is most closely associated with a sense of calling or an orientation toward internalization, several techniques are available to enhance and capitalize on those orientations. Reinforcing the benefits produced for others, associating work outcomes with the core values of employees, identifying the long-term impact created by the work, and emphasizing contribution goals more than achievement goals all foster a sense of meaningfulness and, as a result, higher levels of performance.

ASSESSING POSITIVE LEADERSHIP ACTIVITIES

As a quick assessment of practical leadership activities that enable positive meaning, the following diagnostic questions may be helpful. Use the following scale to respond.

1 — Never 2 — Seldom 3 — Sometimes
4 — Frequently 5 — Always

As a leader, to what extent do you:

_____ Establish, recognize, reward, and maintain accountability for goals that contribute to human benefit, so that the effects on other people are obvious?

_____ Emphasize and reinforce the core values of the individuals who work in the organization, so that congruence between what the organization accomplishes and what people value is transparent?

_____ Tie the outcomes of the work to an extended time frame, so that long-term benefits are clear?

_____ Ensure that contribution goals take precedence over acquisition or achievement goals for individuals in the organization?

6

Implementing Positive Strategies

Some individuals have appropriately questioned whether positive leadership is merely a whitewash of serious leadership challenges. They conclude that positive leadership is too "touchy-feely," or that positive leadership strategies are not appropriate when serious challenges arise, when people are cynical, or when the environment is not benevolent. Moreover, some conclude that positive leadership is, after all, merely a product of a happy countenance, an optimistic outlook, or a charismatic personality attribute.

The examples of Rocky Flats, Griffin, and Prudential offered at the beginning of this book, however, illustrate that positive leadership is effective even in the face of the most difficult challenges. Positive leadership *does not* imply that leaders should just smile and that everything will be fine, or only give praise, or avoid competition and beating opponents, or never criticize others, or always avoid the negative, or do not worry about problems and obstacles, or just relax the standards and do not expect too much.

Instead, positive leadership implies even higher standards of performance, more rigorous expectations than normal, and achievement that exceeds by a wide margin customary or average execution. It is not easy to implement, but as pointed out in earlier chapters, abundant empirical evidence suggests that positive leadership produces physiological, cognitive, emotional, social, and work-related advantages. Organizations do better when positive leadership is present (see Cameron & Spreitzer, 2012).

Being convinced that this is true, however, still leaves a challenge of implementing positive leadership strategies in organizations populated by skeptical, or uninformed, individuals. Therefore, this chapter introduces a tool that can assist leaders in implementing the positive strategies discussed in the first five chapters.

One of the most helpful techniques leaders can use to implement the four strategies of positive leadership is a process referred to as the Personal Management Interview (PMI) program. This technique is applicable in professional settings with leaders and subordinates, in families with parents and children, and in volunteer settings such as spiritually based organizations or community service groups. The PMI program provides a straightforward way to institutionalize the four positive strategies on an ongoing basis.

These four strategies are most effectively applied when specific interactions between leaders and their subordinates are planned and conducted frequently. Whereas leaders usually have good intentions to facilitate a positive climate, positive relationships, positive communication, and positive meaning, the press of everyday problems often drives out the best of intentions. One attribute of positive leaders, however, is that they provide others with opportunities to receive regular feedback, feel supported and bolstered, and be coached, counseled, and developed. Providing these opportunities is difficult because of the time demands most leaders face. The PMI program is designed to address this concern.

In research conducted among intact teams—such as project teams, top-management teams, consulting teams, and departmental groups—the implementation of a PMI program significantly improved the performance of these teams on both subjective factors such as morale, trust, and engagement and objective factors such as productivity and goal accomplishment (Boss, 1983). Teams that implemented PMI programs, for example, significantly improved their performance over time, whereas teams that did not implement them remained the same. Teams that initially implemented PMI programs and then stopped the programs were also found to significantly improve their performance until cessation of the PMI programs, and then performance deteriorated.

Figure 6.1, for example, shows the performance of two matched sets of teams. Each line in the graph represents five teams whose performance was measured by a combination of objective factors (e.g., productivity, output) and subjective factors (e.g., trust, satisfaction). All of the teams were performing at essentially the same level at the outset of the investigation, and all ten teams initially implemented a PMI program. Each team's performance increased significantly after implementation.

Five of the teams continued to implement PMI programs and were assessed at 6-month intervals over an 18-month time frame. Performance increased and stayed high in these

FIGURE 6.1   Intact Teams' Performance before and after Implementing PMIs

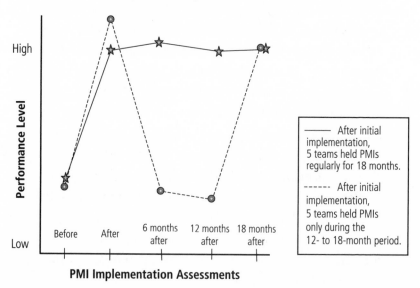

——— After initial implementation, 5 teams held PMIs regularly for 18 months.

------ After initial implementation, 5 teams held PMIs only during the 12- to 18-month period.

PMI Implementation Assessments

(SOURCE: Boss, 1983)

teams. The other five teams, on the other hand, initially implemented PMI programs and then stopped. At the 6- and 12-month points in time, measured performance had fallen to previous levels. After one year, the five teams that ceased their PMI programs were shown the data—what performance levels they had achieved with PMI programs and where they were performing at the present time. These teams reimplemented PMI programs and after six months had significantly improved performance again (Boss, 1983).

Another study compared performance scores—objective and subjective assessments—in five health-care organizations (Goodman & Boss, 2002). Organizational performance scores on objective and subjective factors were significantly higher in each organization when PMI programs were in place compared to when they were not. Importantly, individuals in the organizations were also positively affected by the PMI programs. Employees were categorized into three groups according to the extent to which they felt burned out, overwhelmed, and highly stressed in their work. They were ranked as having high, medium, and low burnout levels. When PMI programs were in place, a majority of employees experienced little if any burnout (53 percent had low burnout scores compared to 29 percent with high burnout scores). When PMI programs were not in place, the larger percentage of employees felt overwhelmed (43 percent had high burnout scores compared to 38 percent with low burnout scores).

The point is that a PMI program appears to have a significant positive impact on team and organizational performance as well as on the personal work experience of individual employees. Empirical evidence suggests that performance improves when a PMI program is implemented, and that individual employees have a more positive experience at work.

IMPLEMENTING A PERSONAL MANAGEMENT INTERVIEW PROGRAM

A PMI program is quite simple in concept as well as in application. It consists of two steps. The first step is to hold a one time only *role-negotiation session*, which is designed to clarify expectations, responsibilities, standards of evaluation, reporting relationships, culture, and values. This psychological contract-setting meeting should be held early in a relationship as a way to establish a foundation of clarity of expectations and a path for moving forward. In a work setting this means holding role-negotiation sessions when new leaders or new direct reports are assigned together. In a family it occurs when children are old enough to understand their responsibilities in the family. In a community-service setting it is scheduled when the group first comes together to accomplish a task.

Unless such a meeting is held, many individuals do not have a definitive idea about what is expected of them in their role or on what basis they will be evaluated. More importantly, the underlying often-undiscussed aspects of their roles are never clarified, such as the values, cultural attributes, and styles that distinguish the setting.

In the informal surveys I have conducted over the last 20 years with thousands of leaders, few reported that they had participated in a role-negotiation session with the person to whom they report. Most leaders merely learn on the job or follow the path of a predecessor. A surprisingly low percentage of leaders express confidence that they know precisely what is expected of them, how they are being evaluated, the measurement criteria being applied, or the full array of resources in place that will allow them to flourish. In a role-negotiation session, that uncertainty is addressed. The mission, goals, and values of the organization are made explicit. The appraisal system, the accountability system, and the rewards are made clear. The leader and each of his or her direct reports negotiate all role-related issues that are not prescribed by policy or by mandate. A relationship of mutual understanding and mutual commitment is formed. Importantly, a written record is made of the agreements and responsibilities that result from the meeting. Keeping a written account serves as an informal contract between the leader and the direct report, and it ensures that the meeting really need only occur on a one-time basis.

The goal of a role-negotiation session is simply to obtain clarity between both parties regarding what each expects from the other, what the goals and standards are, and what the ground rules are for the relationship and for task accomplishment. Goal clarity is an important prerequisite for high performance (Locke & Latham, 2002), and this role-negotiation meeting helps provide that clarity. It

TABLE 6.1 Examples of Role-Negotiation Session Agenda Items

A psychological contract is established.
The focus is on clarifying detailed expectations of one another, including:
Role performance
Areas of responsibility
Accountability and rewards
Interpersonal relationships
Mission, goals, and values
Clear agreements regarding performance are established.
Nonnegotiable issues are identified and justified.
A written account of the results of the session is made available to both participants.
Results of the session are shared with those who will be affected by the agreements.

provides a foundation on which the relationship can be built and helps facilitate better performance on the part of the leader as well as the direct report. Because this role negotiation is not adversarial in tone but, rather, focuses on mutual support and positivity, the four positive strategies should characterize the interaction. PMIs help develop a positive climate, form a positive relationship, reinforce positive communication, and clarify the positive meaning associated with the work. Table 6.1 outlines examples of agenda items for the role-negotiation session.

ONGOING ONE-ON-ONE PMIs

The second, and most important, step in a PMI program is to hold ongoing, *one-on-one meetings* between the leader and each direct report. These meetings are regular (not just when a mistake is made or when a crisis arises), one-on-one, and face-to-face (not staff meetings, luncheon dates, or electronic messages). Successful positive leaders always hold these meetings at least monthly, if not more frequently. Seldom does this strategy work when frequency is less than monthly. Frequent PMIs are important both in organizations and in families. Many times, of course, leaders choose to hold PMIs more frequently than monthly, depending on the life-cycle rhythms of their work and the time pressures they face.

PMIs are not department staff meetings, family gatherings, or end-of-the-day checkups. They occur one-on-one with sufficient time to accomplish very specific objectives. These include generating action steps focused on performance improvement and relationship building. The meeting provides the two people with a chance to communicate freely, openly, and collaboratively. It also provides leaders with the opportunity to coach and develop subordinates and to help them improve their own skills or job performance. It presents an opportunity to demonstrate and reinforce behaviors that enable positive climates, positive communication, positive relationships, and positive meaning.

A PMI is a collaborative meeting—not a top-down, micromanagement mechanism—so both persons prepare agenda items for the meeting in advance, work together to make progress, and leave the experience both personally and interpersonally uplifted. Rather than being an attempt to tightly control people, this meeting becomes a means to foster collaboration, information sharing, and mutual benefit. It is a means to implement the four strategies that characterize positive leadership.

Each PMI meeting usually requires from 45 to 60 minutes and focuses on problem-solving issues as well as positive strategies. Items typically on the agenda include the following:

- leadership and organizational issues
- information sharing
- interpersonal issues
- obstacles to improvement
- training in necessary skills
- individual needs
- feedback on job performance and on personal capabilities
- resource needs
- accountability for commitments made in past meetings
- targets and goals
- career development
- personal concerns or problems

A PMI is a working meeting that leads to verifiable improvements. It is a crucial means by which individuals and organizations accomplish their tasks in a way that can produce positive deviance. It is task focused as well as relationship focused.

The PMI meeting is not just a time to sit and chat. It has two overarching—and crucial—objectives: (1) to foster improvement in performance, and (2) to strengthen positive climates, positive relationships, positive communication, and positive meaning. If performance improvement does not occur as a result of the meeting, it is not being held correctly. If the positive strategies are not strengthened over time, something is not working as it should.

The PMI meeting always leads toward identifying action items that need to be accomplished before the next meeting, some by the direct report and others by the leader. These action items are articulated and clarified at the end of the meeting and reviewed again at the beginning of the next meeting. Accountability is maintained for improvement. Action, not just talk, is the explicit goal. Table 6.2 summarizes some potential agenda items for the PMI sessions.

A PMI is not just a meeting held because it is on the calendar. Without agreements as to specific actions that will be taken, and the accountability that will be maintained, it will be a waste of time for both parties. It is not a meeting just because someone scheduled it. It takes priority because it is the means by which positively deviant performance is achieved.

Sometimes PMIs are confused with the normal performance appraisal process mandated in most organizations. PMIs are *not* formal appraisal sessions conducted by the leader. Rather, they are development and improvement

TABLE 6.2	Examples of Agenda Items for PMI Sessions
Major goals:	
	Continuous improvement
	Team building and personal development
	Feedback
	Reinforce positive climates, positive relationships, positive communication, and positive meaning
First agenda item is to follow up on action items from the previous PMI session	
Major agenda items include:	
	Organizational and job issues
	Information sharing
	Training and development
	Resource needs
	Interpersonal issues
	Obstacles to improvement
	Targets and goals
	Appraisal and feedback
	Career development
	Personal issues
	A supportive, nonpunitive environment
	Advanced preparation of agenda items by both parties
	Accountability required of both parties
	Training of participants in advance
Last agenda item is to review action items arising from the session	

sessions in which both the leader and the direct report have a stake. They do not replace formal performance appraisal sessions, but they supplement them. The purpose of PMIs is not to conduct monthly evaluations or appraisals. Instead, PMIs provide an opportunity for individuals to spend personal time with their leaders to work out issues, report information, experience a positive environment, develop personal capabilities, provide and receive feedback, and improve performance. This implies that both the leader and the direct report prepare for the meeting, and both bring agenda items to be discussed.

When held successfully, PMIs help eliminate unscheduled interruptions and long, inefficient group meetings. At each subsequent PMI, action items are reviewed from previous meetings so that continuous improvement and accountability are expected. PMIs become an institutionalized, continuous-improvement activity, a key to building the collaboration and teamwork needed in organizations, and an effective mechanism to implement the strategies that produce positive climates, positive relationships, positive communication, and positive meaning.

OBJECTIONS

The major objection to holding PMI sessions, of course, is lack of time. Most leaders are of the opinion that they simply cannot impose on their schedules a series of one-on-one meetings with each of their team members, direct reports, or children. If a leader has seven or eight direct reports, for example, this requires seven or eight hours a month of face-to-face meetings, plus preparation time.

Boss's (1983) research found, however, that a variety of benefits resulted when a PMI program was instituted, and one of the most important was time savings. Leaders found that as a result of holding PMIs, more discretionary time became available to them than before implementing the program. This is because the PMI program reduced interruptions, unscheduled meetings, mistakes, and problem-solving time, and it increased alignment, collaboration, improvement strategies, goal clarity, accountability, and positive energy. On the average, leaders freed up the equivalent of almost a day a month in discretionary time as a result of the benefits produced by the PMI program.

Some flexibility may be required, of course, in different settings and in different organizations. PMIs with family members are not of the same character as PMIs in a work setting. Moreover, a number of variations have been reported by leaders who were committed to holding PMIs but who faced unusual working situations. One leader found that it was more important for him to hold PMIs with peers—across divisions and functions—than to hold the meetings with direct reports. His coordination requirements were far greater with colleagues than with individuals who reported to him. In his case, PMIs were peer-to-peer.

Another leader had almost 50 direct reports, which made one-on-one meetings on a monthly basis impossible. She identified a "kitchen cabinet" of eight or nine individuals with whom she scheduled PMI meetings. She judged this group to be the rainmakers, high potentials, and central influencers in her unit, and PMIs with this group produced the greatest performance impact.

Still another leader with a large number of direct reports asked her team to nominate individuals who would serve as representatives of subgroups within the unit. PMIs were held with these representatives, and then the representatives held PMIs with others in their group. Another regional sales manager located in Ethiopia had direct reports in Singapore, Taipei, Tokyo, Seoul, and Manila, which made monthly face-to-face meetings impractical. He scheduled an hour-long telephone call monthly, and then on a quarterly basis one or the other flew to hold a face-to-face PMI on site. In each case, the benefits of PMIs made the investment in a creative solution worthwhile.

The point is, both empirical evidence and practical experience provide a strong case that PMIs produce performance improvements and, in addition, become a successful experience in themselves. They are a means by which individuals experience the positive outcomes associated with the four positive leadership strategies, as well as increase organizational effectiveness, individual accountability, department meeting efficiency, and individual development. Even when correction or negative feedback needs to be communicated, when obstacles must be overcome, and when challenges or crises are faced, a PMI program provides an effective way to address those issues in a positively deviant way.

SUMMARY

Leaders can implement the four strategies of positive leadership—enabling positive climates, positive relationships, positive communication, and positive meaning—by engaging in a Personal Management Interview program. This begins by holding a one-time role-negotiation session with each direct report, designed to establish a psychological contract that helps clarify goals, expectations, important cultural attributes, and areas of responsibility. Abundant evidence shows that goal clarity is an important prerequisite for high performance (Locke & Latham, 2002), and this role-negotiation meeting helps provide that clarity.

The role-negotiation session is followed by ongoing, one-on-one, face-to-face, at-least-monthly meetings designed to facilitate positive climates, positive relationships, and positive communication and to clarify positive meaning. These ongoing meetings between a leader and each of his or her direct reports not only help leaders implement the four strategies of positive leadership, but a variety of additional benefits also accrue. These include institutionalizing continuous improvement, maintaining accountability, developing personal competencies, and establishing a two-way exchange of feedback. Empirical investigations support the strong positive connection between holding PMIs and significant improvement in both organizational and individual performance.

ASSESSING POSITIVE LEADERSHIP ACTIVITIES

As a quick assessment of practical leadership activities that enable a PMI program, the following diagnostic questions may be helpful. Use the following scale to respond.

**1 — Never 2 — Seldom 3 — Sometimes
4 — Frequently 5 — Always**

As a leader, to what extent do you:

_____ Clarify for your direct reports the specific set of expectations and responsibilities associated with their roles, as well as the mission, values, and culture of the organization?

_____ Meet at least monthly in one-on-one meetings with your direct reports?

_____ Consistently and continually emphasize continuous improvement and the development of strong interpersonal relationships among your direct reports?

_____ Have a formalized routine (such as PMIs) in which you can regularly demonstrate positive climates, positive relationships, positive communication, and positive meaning associated with the work?

CHAPTER

7

Developing Positive Leadership

General Rhonda Cornum, recently retired head of the U.S. Army's Comprehensive Soldier Fitness program, was on a search-and-rescue flight in Iraq in 1991 when her Blackhawk helicopter was shot down. Five of the eight crew members were killed. Cornum and two others were taken prisoner by the Iraqi army.

"Let me tell you something about my own experience," she said. "So I got shot down. The next thing I know some Iraqi soldier is dislocating the shoulder in my already broken arm. I thought, 'Well, I'm not dead. I'm a prisoner of war.' As we were crashing, I remember thinking that I had two options—either I'd be dead or I'd be captured. Being captured was better. I could still wiggle my fingers, and that was good, because I knew we were really good at doing orthopedics. Then this guy put a gun at the back of my head, and I realized that this was not going to go very well. So I decided to think of something positive. I was really wracking my brain trying to come up with something. I thought, 'Well, I've had a chance to have a great life; I've had a great husband and a great kid; I've had the chance to do a lot of really great things; and at least it won't hurt, which is a better end than a lot of people get.' Then I heard the gun go 'click,' and I thought, 'Well, this really isn't that bad'" (Horrigan, 2010).

Cornum recounted her experiences in her book *She Went to War* (1993) and dismissed her sexual assault by her Iraqi captors as "not the biggest deal of my life." But the most important message she conveyed was this: *Being positive is teachable.* Positive leadership is not inherent and can be learned by anyone (see also Cornum, Matthews, & Seligman, 2011).

This book offers summaries of empirical investigations as well as examples from positively deviant organizations that provide evidence for the same conclusion espoused by Cornum: Leaders can learn to be positive and can produce extraordinary performance.

On the other hand, because negative phenomena tend to dominate people's attention, and because human beings have learned to pay more attention to potential harm than to potential benefit, positive leadership is not the most common form of leadership. It represents an aberration from the norm. It is unlikely to emerge without conscious effort and attention. People have learned that ignoring negative feedback can be dangerous. Thus leaders' attention tends to focus on problematic, threatening, or potentially harmful phenomena rather than on positive phenomena (Cameron, 2008).

Similarly, organizational processes and routines are usually developed to avoid errors, to prevent or address problems, and to reduce or eliminate deviance. It is normal in organizations to resist deviance, whether it is positive or negative. The activity of organizing is itself almost always an exercise in reducing variance, that is, creating more predictability, control, and reliability. Organizing, by definition, helps diminish failure (negative deviance) but at the same time extraordinary excellence (positive deviance). If positive leadership is to be pursued, therefore, assiduous attention is required in order to overcome most people's learned sensitivity to the negative.

In previous chapters, four validated leadership strategies were described that are associated with positively deviant outcomes. Each strategy has associated with it at least two specific tools and techniques that represent underutilized but very effective leadership levers.

These four strategies are not independent of each other, of course, and they tend to overlap and interrelate with one another. For example, it is easy to see that positive communication can have powerful effects on positive relationships and positive climates. Positive meaning may strongly affect positive climates and positive communication. Positive relationships help strengthen a sense of positive meaning and positive climates—and so forth. The practices and techniques that operationalize each strategy may also affect other strategies.

Moreover, evidence suggests that implementing a Personal Management Interview program creates a setting in which each of the four strategies may be effectively implemented. Thus employing any of these strategies tends to establish an amplifying effect in the others and helps enable positively deviant outcomes. Amplifying extraordinary performance is the primary aim of positive leadership.

POSITIVE LEADERSHIP PRINCIPLES

The propositions that follow summarize the empirical findings associated with each strategy and are guidelines for leaders who aspire to enable positive deviance in their organizations.

- Positive leaders enable extraordinary performance by fostering a positive work climate.

  Empirical evidence suggests that working in a positive climate has substantial positive effects on individual and organizational performance. Among the leadership enablers that affect the work climate are fostering (1) compassion, (2) forgiveness, and (3) expressions of gratitude at work.

  Expressing compassion involves noticing that pain has been experienced, expressing care and concern, and organizing systematic action to help repair damage or support the person who is suffering. Facilitating forgiveness involves acknowledging the hurt, identifying a purpose to which employees can look forward, maintaining high expectations or standards of performance, providing support for harmed persons, letting go of feelings of offense and grudges, and legitimizing the use of language that elevates thought and communicates virtuousness. Frequent and public expressions of gratitude to others can be enhanced as individuals are encouraged to keep gratitude journals, recording things for which they are grateful each day, engage in purposeful gratitude visits in which the agenda is simply to convey thanks to another person, or distribute gratitude messages where cards or notes are provided to individuals who deserve appreciation.

Such expressions lead people toward more respectful and supportive relationships, which, in turn, affect organizational performance. Leaders who enable the expression of these virtues create a climate in which people are cared for, supported, and encouraged to flourish. Such a climate is associated with positive physiological effects, mental and emotional effects, and organizational performance effects.

- Positive leaders enable extraordinary performance by fostering positive relationships among members.

Empirical evidence suggests that experiencing positive interpersonal relationships produces an array of positive physiological, mental, social, and emotional benefits for individuals and elevated performance for organizations. Making contributions to relationships more than receiving benefits from relationships is the main factor that produces positive outcomes. Among the important but less common leadership strategies for engendering positive relationships are (1) developing and managing positive energy networks and (2) capitalizing on employees' strengths and best-self attributes.

In addition to radiating positive energy themselves, positive leaders identify individuals who contribute positive energy to others around them, and they enable these people to infuse the organization with this energy. They facilitate the building of positive energy networks, positive mentoring relations, and positive energy teams. These positive energy networks strengthen interpersonal relationships, foster coordination and collaboration, and enhance the efficiency of interactions so that performance advantages for individuals and organizations result.

Similarly, positive leaders emphasize and build on employees' strengths (what they do well) rather than focus on their weaknesses, and this emphasis creates an attraction to forming strong interpersonal ties. Addressing weaknesses helps people achieve a level of basic competence, but building on strengths helps people achieve excellence in performance and in relationships.

- Positive leaders enable extraordinary performance by fostering positive communication.

Empirical evidence suggests that an abundance of positive communication compared to negative communication is related to higher levels of organizational performance and connectivity among people. Five positive statements for every negative statement will predict flourishing in organizations and families. Engagement, information exchange, and commitment are enhanced in the presence of positive communication. Among the many strategies that may foster positive communication are the use of (1) best-self feedback and (2) supportive communication.

The best-self feedback process builds on the power of positive feedback by helping individuals systematically gather information about their own strengths and unique contributions. Because most people have difficulty accurately identifying their own strengths, using others' descriptions of the unique value that they produced or a special contribution that was made allows them to capitalize on what they do best. Creating a best-self portrait, or a description of their strengths and the conditions under which they add significant value, helps them reproduce the circumstances in which their best contributions can be made.

Using supportive communication—especially congruent, descriptive, and problem-centered statements— allows leaders to provide corrective or negative feedback in ways that make the communication encouraging and helpful, strengthening rather than weakening the relationship, and enhancing individual performance. The negative effects of criticism are avoided and replaced with a trusting, supportive relationship. Positive communication, in other words, builds on positive energy and positive regard, which are strongly related to high levels of effectiveness among individuals and organizations.

- Positive leaders enable extraordinary performance by associating the work being done with positive meaning.

Empirical evidence suggests that when people experience positive meaning in their work—or a sense of calling—performance is elevated and individual well-being is enhanced. Leaders enhance the meaningfulness of the task in at least four ways:

(1) Identifying the positive impact that the work produces on the well-being of people fosters meaningfulness. The more human impact that can be observed—that is, how the work affects individuals for the better—the more meaningful the work. The more meaningful the work, the more individuals desire to share its effects with other people.

(2) Associating the work with a virtue or an important personal value engenders positive meaning. Highlighting the relationship between work and sustainability, generosity, or compassion, for example, helps engender meaningfulness. Identifying a higher purpose that supersedes personal benefit is almost always a prerequisite to prosocial and contributory work activities.

(3) Identifying the long-term effects of the work beyond immediate outcomes, and highlighting the ripple effect that may occur, also enhances positive meaning. Leaving a legacy that benefits people beyond the immediate circumstances represents a form of unselfishness that is associated with high levels of performance.

(4) Building supportive relationships and a sense of community among coworkers also enhances positive meaning. Leaders who highlight and pursue contribution goals as opposed to self-interest goals enable important individual and organizational outcomes such as learning, trust, high-quality connections, and improved performance.

- Positive leaders enable extraordinary performance by implementing these four strategies through a Personal Management Interview program.

Empirical evidence suggests that the implementation of a PMI program leads to significant increases in organizational and individual performance. When PMIs are implemented, performance improves. When PMIs are halted, organizational performance tends to deteriorate. Similarly, in comparing organizations with and without PMI programs in place, individuals experience significantly less stress and overload when PMIs are held compared to when they are not.

A PMI program is implemented by holding an initial, one-time, role-negotiation session, followed by an ongoing, regularly scheduled, one-on-one meeting with each direct report. These meetings provide the formalized process by which positive climates, positive relationships, positive communication, and positive meaning can be developed and demonstrated. Rather than increasing the time burden on leaders, PMIs have been demonstrated to actually increase discretionary time so that leaders are more efficient as well as more effective.

In sum, while not ignoring or minimizing problems and obstacles, leaders who enable positive deviance focus on engendering that which is elevating and virtuous in organizations. Because this positive emphasis is contrary to the natural tendencies of most leaders, specific strategies have been identified that can foster human flourishing and unusually high positive levels of performance. Four interrelated strategies for positive leaders have been discussed, and research associated with each has been reviewed in order to validate the prescriptions. These four strategies are not comprehensive, of course, but they illustrate relatively unique, empirically verified enablers available to leaders.

The four strategies have *amplifying* effects on one another. As mentioned, positive climates tend to foster positive relationships and communication, positive meaning facilitates positive climates and relationships, positive relationships foster positive communication and positive climates, and positive communication fosters positive climates and positive relationships. As a way to help leaders get started on this amplifying process and implement some of these strategies, this final section provides a simple tool for identifying two or three positive leadership behaviors that can be initiated right away.

PERSONALIZING POSITIVE LEADERSHIP STRATEGIES

Implementing positive leadership strategies should be tailored, of course, to the specific circumstances in which leaders lead. Being a positive leader in the family may require different behaviors than being a positive leader on a project team or in a manufacturing division. Positive leadership in Western Europe may need to be implemented differently than positive leadership in Southeast Asia. Moreover, some positive leadership behaviors may already be institutionalized in an organization, whereas others may be entirely neglected. Personal style, cultural norms, and organizational expectations must all be taken into account in implementing specific techniques and tools.

A two-step process is offered in the interest of helping leaders identify some specific behaviors they can implement in becoming more positive. The two steps are (1) diagnosing current leadership behaviors and (2) identifying specific actions that help implement the four positive leadership strategies.

Step 1: Diagnosing current practice

A consolidated assessment instrument is provided in Table 7.1, which summarizes the behaviors discussed in each of the preceding chapters. Individuals can identify the extent to which they engage in these behaviors as part of their normal leadership activities. Since improvement cannot occur unless reasonably accurate self-assessments

TABLE 7.1 Positive Leadership Assessment As a leader, to what extent do you:	1 = Never	2 = Seldom	3 = Sometimes	4 = Frequently	5 = Always
1. Foster information sharing so that people become aware of colleagues' difficulties and, therefore, can express compassion?					
2. Encourage the public expression of compassion by sponsoring formal events to communicate emotional support?					
3. Demonstrate forgiveness for mistakes and errors rather than punish perpetrators or hold grudges?					
4. Provide support and development as an indicator of forgiveness for individuals who have blundered?					
5. Express gratitude to multiple employees each day?					
6. Make gratitude visits and the distribution of gratitude notes a daily practice?					
7. Ensure that employees have an opportunity to provide emotional, intellectual, or physical support *to* others in addition to receiving support *from* the organization?					
8. Model positive energy yourself, and also recognize and encourage other positive energizers in your organization?					
9. Diagnose your organization's energy networks so that you support and utilize individuals in energy hubs as well as help develop peripheral members?					
10. Provide more feedback to individuals about their strengths rather than their weaknesses?					
11. Spend more time with your strongest performers than with your weakest performers?					
12. Communicate a ratio of approximately five positive messages for every negative message to those with whom you interact?					
13. Provide opportunities for employees to receive best-self feedback and develop best-self portraits?					

TABLE 7.1 (continued) Positive Leadership Assessment	1 = Never	2 = Seldom	3 = Sometimes	4 = Frequently	5 = Always
As a leader, to what extent do you:					
14. Consistently distribute notes or cards to your employees complimenting their performance?					
15. Provide negative feedback in supportive ways—especially using descriptive rather than evaluative statements—so that the relationship is strengthened?					
16. Focus on the detrimental *behavior* and its consequences, not on the person, when correcting people or providing negative feedback?					
17. Establish, recognize, reward, and maintain accountability for goals that contribute to human benefit so that the effects on other people are obvious?					
18. Emphasize and reinforce the core values of the individuals who work in the organization so that congruence between what the organization accomplishes and what people value is transparent?					
19. Tie the outcomes of the work to an extended time frame so that long-term benefits are clear?					
20. Ensure that contribution goals take precedence over acquisition goals for individuals in the organization?					
21. Clarify for your direct reports the specific set of expectations and responsibilities associated with their roles, as well as the mission, values, and culture of the organization?					
22. Meet at least monthly in one-on-one meetings with your direct reports?					
23. Consistently and continually emphasize continuous improvement and the development of strong interpersonal relationships among your direct reports?					
24. Have a formalized routine (such as PMIs) in which you can regularly demonstrate positive climates, positive relationships, positive communication, and positive meaning associated with the work?					

occur, a realistic evaluation of current (not desired) performance is a prerequisite.

In reviewing this self-assessment, individuals should identify the areas in which they are doing especially well (scores of 4 and 5) as well as the areas in which they would like to improve (scores of 1 and 2). It is important that leaders highlight and capitalize on strengths as well as identify areas that may require upgrading. Effective positive leaders score in the 3, 4, and 5 range on these items, with an average rating of 4.

Step 2: Planning for implementation

Based on the current levels of positive leadership behaviors, individuals should identify two or three behaviors that can have a significant impact on improving positive leadership. Since it is unlikely that more than two or three items can be effectively changed, a focused, prioritized list of key behaviors should be targeted. The question is *What two or three actions can I take that will enhance my effectiveness in each of the five positive leadership strategies?*

Leaders may want to check the specific behaviors on which they will focus as they attempt to foster positive climates, positive relationships, positive communication, and positive meaning. Of course, the list of suggestions in Table 7.2 is not comprehensive, so other behaviors may also be identified that can foster positively deviant outcomes.

In selecting items to implement, individuals may want to respond to two different circumstances—their personal or family life (e.g., in relation to home life, friendships, volunteer activities) and their professional or work life (e.g., in

Positive Leadership Strategy	Personal or Family Life	Professional or Work Life
TABLE 7.2 Implementing Positive Leadership		
Encourage compassion		
Notice and share information		
Express emotions and feelings		
Enable appropriate compassionate responses		
Encourage forgiveness		
Acknowledge harm		
Identify a positive purpose		
Maintain high standards		
Provide personal support		
Use forgiving language		
Encourage gratitude		
Conduct gratitude visits		
Write gratitude letters		
Keep a gratitude journal		
Foster positive energy		
Provide opportunities for serving others		
Personally model positive energy		
Diagnose the unit's energy network		
Recognize and reinforce positive energizers		
Manage negative energizers in stages		
Capitalize on others' strengths		
Spend time with the strongest performers		
Provide opportunities for others to do what they do best		
Frequently celebrate positive outcomes		

(continued)

TABLE 7.2 Implementing Positive Leadership (continued)		
Positive Leadership Strategy	Personal or Family Life	Professional or Work Life
Provide best-self feedback		
Obtain information from associates on unique personal contributions		
Help others develop a best-self portrait—when they are at their best		
Utilize strength recognition cards		
Use supportive communication		
Provide five positive statements for every negative piece of feedback		
Habitually use supportive communication		
Use descriptive statements in providing negative feedback		
Remain problem- not person-focused in providing negative feedback		
Enhance the meaningfulness of the work		
Identify the work's direct impact on other people		
Associate the work with a core personal value		
Clarify the long-term effects of what is being accomplished		
Reinforce contribution goals more than achievement goals		
Implement Personal Management Interviews		
Hold a role-negotiation meeting with direct reports		
Hold regularly scheduled, one-on-one meetings with direct reports		
Provide regular personal-development opportunities for direct reports		
Ensure regular accountability for continuous improvement		

relation to work colleagues, subordinates, customers). Each setting may require a different set of improvement initiatives.

Again, leaders will want to narrow the items they personally checked in Table 7.2 and select only two or three high-priority behaviors that will produce the highest impact on positive leadership effectiveness. These behaviors should be applied first to the relationships about which leaders care most deeply and which will have the highest impact. Achieving extraordinary performance is the objective of these strategies, and abundant empirical evidence exists suggesting that a few positive leadership strategies can significantly enhance the probability that positively deviant results will occur. Amplifying effects can be instigated with a few well-chosen positive leadership behaviors.

In sum, positive leadership is an aspiration that almost every individual can achieve, and the advantages of such an approach can be remarkable. The statement by the Nobel Laureate Desmond Tutu highlights why positive leadership is so advantageous in a world in which it is quite rare (Tutu, 1999: 263):

> The world is hungry for goodness and it recognizes it when it sees it—and has incredible responses to the good. There is something in all of us that hungers after the good and true, and when we glimpse it in people, we applaud them for it. We long to be just like them.

For more information regarding positive leadership and positive organizational scholarship, visit www.bus.umich.edu/positive or www.centerforpos.org.

References

Algoe, S. B., & Fredrickson, B. L. (2011). Emotional fitness and the movement of affective science from lab to field. *American Psychologist*, *66*, 35–42.

Ancona, D., & Isaacs, W. (2007). Structural balance in teams. In J. E. Dutton & B. R. Ragins (Eds.), *Exploring positive relationships at work* (pp. 225–242). Mahwah, NJ: Erlbaum.

Aristotle. *Metaphysics XII*, 3–4, 7.

Ashforth, B. E., & Kreiner, G. E. (1999). How can you do it? Dirty work and the challenge of constructing a positive identity. *Academy of Management Review*, *24*(3), 413–434.

Bagozzi, R. P. (2003). Positive and negative emotions in organizations. In K. Cameron, J. E. Dutton, & R. E. Quinn (Eds.), *Positive organizational scholarship* (pp. 176–193). San Francisco: Berrett-Koehler.

Baker, W. (2000). *Achieving success through social capital*. San Francisco: Jossey-Bass.

Baker, W. (2004). Half-baked brown bag presentation on positive energy networks. Unpublished manuscript, University of Michigan Business School.

Baker, W., Cross, R., & Parker, A. (2003). What creates energy in organizations? *Sloan Management Review*, *44*, 51–56.

Baker, W., Cross, R., & Wooten, M. (2003). Positive organizational network analysis and energizing relationships. In K. S. Cameron, J. E. Dutton, & R. E. Quinn (Eds.), *Positive organizational scholarship* (pp. 328–342). San Francisco: Berrett-Koehler.

Baker, W., & Dutton, J. E. (2007). Enabling positive social capital in organizations. In J. E. Dutton & B. R. Ragins (Eds.), *Exploring positive relationships at work* (pp. 325–346). Mahwah, NJ: Erlbaum.

Bargh, J. A., & Chartrand, T. L. (1999). The unbearable automaticity of being. *American Psychologist*, *54*(7), 462–479.

Barnard, C. (1968). *The functions of an executive*. Cambridge, MA: Harvard University Press.

Baumeister, R. F. (1991). *Meanings of life*. New York: Guilford Press.

Baumeister, R. F., Bratslavsky, E., Finkenauer, C., & Vohs, K. D. (2001). Bad is stronger than good. *Review of General Psychology*, *5*(4), 323–370.

Baumeister, R. F., & Vohs, K. D. (2002). The pursuit of meaningfulness in life. In C. R. Snyder & S. J. Lopez (Eds.), *Handbook of positive psychology* (pp. 608–618). New York: Oxford University Press.

Bellah, R. N., Madsen, R., Sullivan, W. M., Swidler, A., & Tipton, S. M. (1985). *Habits of the heart: Individualism and commitment in American life*. New York: Harper & Row.

Berkman, L. F., Leo-Summers, L., & Horowitz, R. I. (2002). Emotional support and survival after myocardial infarction: A prospective, population-based study of the elderly. In J. T. Cacioppo et al. (Eds.), *Foundations in social neuroscience* (pp. 314–333). Cambridge, MA: MIT Press.

Blatt, R., & Camden, C. T. (2007). Positive relationships and cultivating community. In J. E. Dutton & B. R. Ragins (Eds.), *Exploring positive relationships at work* (pp. 243–264). Mahwah, NJ: Erlbaum.

Bolino, M. C., Turnley, W. H., & Bloodgood, J. M. (2002). Citizenship behavior and the creation of social capital in organizations. *Academy of Management Review, 27*, 505–522.

Boss, W. L. (1983). Team building and the problem of regression: The personal management interview as an intervention. *Journal of Applied Behavioral Science, 19*, 67–83.

Bostock, S., Hamer, M., Wawrzyniak, A. J., Mitchell, E. S., & Steptoe, A. (2011). Positive emotional style and subjective, cardiovascular, and cortisol responses to acute laboratory stress. *Psychneuroendocrinology, 36*, 1175–1183.

Bright, D., Cameron, K., & Caza, A. (2006). The amplifying and buffering effects of virtuousness in downsized organizations. *Journal of Business Ethics, 64*, 249–269.

Bright, D. S. (2006). Forgiveness as an attribute of leadership. In E. D. Hess & K. S. Cameron (Eds.), *Leading with values: Positivity, virtue, and high performance* (pp. 172–193). Cambridge: Cambridge University Press.

Brondolo, E., Rieppi, R., Erickson, S. A., Bagiella, E., Shapiro, P. A., McKinley, P., & Sloan, R. P. (2003). Hostility, interpersonal interactions, and ambulatory blood pressure. *Psychosomatic Medicine, 65*, 1003–1011.

Brown, S. L., & Brown, R. M. (2006). Selective investment theory: Recasting the functional significance of close relationships. *Psychological Inquiry, 17*, 1–19.

Brown, S. L., Nesse, R. M., Vinokur, A. D., & Smith, D. M. (2003). Providing social support may be better than receiving it: Results from a prospective study. *Psychological Science, 14*, 320–327.

Bruner, J. S., & Goodnow, J. J. (1956). *A study of thinking*. New York: Wiley.

Buckingham, M., & Clifton, D. (2001). *Now, discover your strengths*. New York: Free Press.

Burt, R. (1992). *Structural holes*. Cambridge, MA: Harvard Business School Press.

Cameron, K. S. (1994). Strategies for successful organizational downsizing. *Human Resource Management Journal, 33*, 89–112.

Cameron, K. S. (1998). Strategic organizational downsizing: An extreme case. *Research in Organizational Behavior, 20*, 185–229.

Cameron, K. S. (2003). Organizational virtuousness and performance. In K. S. Cameron, J. E. Dutton, & R. E. Quinn (Eds.), *Positive organizational scholarship* (pp. 48–65). San Francisco: Berrett-Koehler.

Cameron, K. S. (2008). Paradox in positive organizational change. *Journal of Applied Behavioral Science, 44,* 7–24.

Cameron, K. S. (2011). Building relationships by communicating supportively. In D. A. Whetten & K. S. Cameron (Eds.), *Developing management skills* (pp. 233–278). Upper Saddle River, NJ: Prentice Hall.

Cameron, K. S., Bright, D., & Caza, A. (2004). Exploring the relationships between organizational virtuousness and performance. *American Behavioral Scientist, 47*(6), 766–790.

Cameron, K. S., & Caza, A. (2002). Organizational and leadership virtues and the role of forgiveness. *Journal of Leadership and Organizational Studies, 9*(1), 33–48.

Cameron, K. S., & Caza, A. (2004). Contributions to the discipline of positive organizational scholarship. *American Behavioral Scientist, 47,* 731–739.

Cameron, K. S., Dutton, J. E., & Quinn, R. E. (Eds.). (2003). *Positive organizational scholarship.* San Francisco: Berrett-Koehler.

Cameron, K. S., Kim, M. U., & Whetten, D. A. (1987). Organizational effects of decline and turbulence. *Administration Science Quarterly, 32,* 222–240.

Cameron, K. S., & Lavine, M. (2006). *Making the impossible possible.* San Francisco: Berrett-Koehler.

Cameron, K. S., & Plews, E. (in press). Positive leadership in action. *Organizational Dynamics.*

Cameron, K. S., & Spreitzer, G. M. (2012). *Oxford handbook of positive organizational scholarship.* New York: Oxford University Press.

Casey, G. W. (2011). Comprehensive soldier fitness: A vision for psychological resilience in the U.S. Army. *American Psychologist, 66,* 1–3.

Caza, A., & Cameron, K. S. (2008). Positive organizational scholarship: What does it achieve? In C. L. Cooper & S. Clegg (Eds.), *Handbook of macro-organizational behavior* (pp. 99–116). New York: Sage.

Chappell, T. (1999). *Managing upside down: The seven intentions of value-centered leadership.* Boston: William Morrow.

Chen, G. (2007). *Subject-object meaningfulness in knowledge work.* Unpublished honors thesis, Organizational Studies Program, University of Michigan.

Chida, Y., & Steptoe, A. (2008). Positive psychological well-being and mortality: A quantitative review of prospective observational studies. *Psychosomatic Medicine, 70,* 741–756.

Clifton, D. O., & Harter, J. K. (2003). Investing in strengths. In K. S. Cameron, J. E. Dutton, & R. E. Quinn (Eds.), *Positive organizational scholarship* (pp. 111–121). San Francisco: Berrett-Koehler.

Cohen, S., Doyle, W. J., Skoner, D., Rabin, B. S., & Gwaltney, J. M. (1997). Social ties and susceptibility to the common cold. *Journal of the American Medical Association, 277,* 1940–1944.

Collins, J. (2001). *Good to great.* New York: HarperCollins.

Conger, J. A. (1989). *Servant leadership: Behind the mystique of exceptional leadership.* San Francisco: Jossey-Bass.

Cook, J., & Wall, T. D. (1980). New work attitude measures of trust, organizational commitment, and personal need non-fulfillment. *Journal of Occupational Psychology, 53,* 39–52.

Cooperrider, D. L., & Srivastva, S. (1987). Appreciative inquiry in organizational life. *Research in Organizational Change and Development, 1,* 129–169.

Cornum, R. (1993). *She went to war.* San Francisco: Presidio Press.

Cornum, R., Matthews, M., & Seligman, M. (2011). Building resilience in a challenging institutional context. *American Psychologist, 66,* 4–9.

Covey, S. R. (2004). *Seven habits of highly effective people.* New York: Free Press.

Crocker, J., Nuer, N., Olivier, M., & Cohen, S. (2006). *Egosystem and ecosystem: Two motivational orientations for the self.* Working paper, Department of Psychology, University of Michigan.

Crocker, J., & Park, L. E. (2004). The costly pursuit of self-esteem. *Psychological Bulletin, 130,* 392–414.

Csikszentmihalyi, M. (1990). *Flow: The psychology of optimal experience.* New York: Harper Perennial.

Denison, D. R. (1996). What *is* the difference between organizational culture and organizational climate? A native's point of view on a decade of paradigm wars. *Academy of Management Review, 21*(3), 619–654.

Dent, N. (1984). *The moral psychology of the virtues.* New York: Cambridge University Press.

Deutschman, A. (2005). Making change. *Fast Company* (May), 52–62.

Diener, E. (1995). Factors predicting the subjective well-being of nations. *Journal of Personality and Social Psychology, 69,* 851–864.

Diener, E., & Biswas-Diener, R. (2008). *Happiness: Unlocking the mysteries of psychological wealth.* Malden, MA: Blackwell.

Dockray, S., & Steptoe, A. (2010). Positive affect and psychobiological processes. *Neuroscience and Biobehavioral Reviews, 35,* 69–75.

Drazin, R., Hess, E. D., & Mihoubi, F. (2006). Synovus Financial Corporation: Just take care of your people. In E. D. Hess & K. S. Cameron (Eds.), *Leading with values* (pp. 9–28). Cambridge: Cambridge University Press.

Dutton, J. E. (2003). *Energizing your workplace: Building and sustaining high quality relationships at work.* San Francisco: Jossey-Bass.

Dutton, J. E., Frost, P. J., Worline, M. C., Lilius, J. M., & Kanov, J. M. (2002). Leading in times of trauma. *Harvard Business Review* (January), 54–61.

Dutton, J. E., & Heaphy, E. D. (2003). The power of high-quality connections. In K. S. Cameron, J. E. Dutton, & R. E. Quinn (Eds.), *Positive organizational scholarship* (pp. 263–278). San Francisco: Berrett-Koehler.

Dutton, J. E., & Ragins, B. R. (2007). *Exploring positive relationships at work.* Mahwah, NJ: Erlbaum.

Dutton, J. E., & Sonenshein, S. (2007). Positive organizational scholarship. In S. Lopez & A. Beauchamps (Eds.), *Encyclopedia of positive psychology* (pp. 737–742). Malden, MA: Blackwell.

Ehrenreich, B. (2009). *Bright-sided: How positive thinking is undermining America.* New York: Henry Holt.

Emmons, R. A. (2003). Acts of gratitude in organizations. In K. S. Cameron, J. E. Dutton, & R. E. Quinn (Eds.), *Positive organizational scholarship* (pp. 81–93). San Francisco: Berrett-Koehler.

Epel, E., McEwen, B. S., & Ickovics, J. R. (1998). Embodying psychological thriving: Physical thriving in response to stress. *Journal of Social Issues, 54*, 301–322.

Esterling, B. A., Kiecolt-Glaser, J. K., Bodnar, J., & Glaser, R. (1994). Chronic stress, social support, and persistent alterations in the natural killer cell response to cytokines in older adults. *Health Psychology, 13*, 291–299.

Fineman, S. (2006). On being positive: Concerns and counterpoints. *Academy of Management Review, 31*(2), 270–291.

Frankl, V. (1959). *Man's search for meaning.* New York: Pocket Books.

Fredrickson, B. L. (1998). What good are positive emotions? *Review of General Psychology, 2*, 300–319.

Fredrickson, B. L. (2001). The role of positive emotions in positive psychology: The broaden-and-build theory of positive emotions. *American Psychologist, 56*, 218–226.

Fredrickson, B. L. (2002). Positive emotions. In C. R. Snyder & S. J. Lopez (Eds.), *Handbook of positive psychology* (pp. 120–134). New York: Oxford University Press.

Fredrickson, B. L. (2003). Positive emotions and upward spirals in organizations. In K. S. Cameron, J. E. Dutton, & R. E. Quinn (Eds.), *Positive organizational scholarship* (pp. 163–175). San Francisco: Berrett-Koehler.

Fredrickson, B. L. (2009). *Positivity.* New York: Crown Books.

Fredrickson, B. L., & Branigan, C. (2001). Positive emotions. In T. J. Mayne & G. A. Bonnano (Eds.), *Emotions: Current issues and future directions* (pp. 123–151). New York: Guilford Press.

Fredrickson, B. L., & Levenson, R. W. (1998). Positive emotions speed recovery from the cardiovascular sequelae of negative emotions. *Cognition and Emotion, 12*, 191–200.

Fredrickson, B. L., & Losada, M. F. (2005). Positive affect and the complex dynamics of human flourishing. *American Psychologist, 60*, 678–686.

Fredrickson, B. L., Mancuso, R. A., Branigan, C., & Tugade, M. M. (2000). The undoing effect of positive emotions. *Motivation and Emotion, 24,* 237–259.

Frost, P. J. (1999). Why compassion counts. *Journal of Management Inquiry, 8,* 127–133.

George, J. M. (1998). Salesperson mood at work: Implications for helping customers. *Journal of Personal Selling and Sales Management, 18,* 23–30.

George, J. M. (2004). Book review of positive organizational scholarship: Foundations of a new discipline. *Administrative Science Quarterly, 49,* 325–330.

Gibb, J. R. (1961). Defensive communication. *Journal of Communication, 11,* 141–148.

Goodman, E. A., & Boss, R. W. (2002). The phase model of burnout and employee turnover. *Journal of Health and Human Resources Administration, 25*(1), 33–47.

Gottman, J. M. (1994). *What predicts divorce: The relationship between marital processes and marital outcomes.* Northampton, MA: Erlbaum.

Grant, A. M. (2007). Relational job design and the motivation to make a prosocial difference. *Academy of Management Review, 32,* 393–417.

Grant, A. M. (2008). Does intrinsic motivation fuel the prosocial fire? Motivational synergy in predicting persistence, performance, and productivity. *Journal of Applied Psychology, 93,* 48–58.

Grant, A. M., Campbell, E. M., Chen, G., Cottone, K., Lapedis, D., & Lee, K. (2007). Impact and the art of motivation maintenance: The effects of contact with beneficiaries on persistent behavior. *Organizational Behavior and Human Decision Processes, 103,* 53–67.

Grant, A. M., Dutton, J. E., & Russo, B. D. (2008). Giving commitment: Employee support programs and the prosocial sensemaking process. *Academy of Management Journal, 51,* 898–918.

Greenleaf, R. K. (1977). *Servant leadership.* Mahwah, NJ: Paulist Press.

Hackman, J. R. (2008). The perils of positivity. *Journal of Organizational Behavior, 30,* 309–319.

Hackman, J. R., & Oldham, G. R. (1980). *Work design.* Reading, MA: Addison-Wesley.

Hansen, A. L., Johnsen, B. H., & Thayer, J. F. (2003). Vagal influence in the regulation of attention and working memory. *International Journal of Psychophysiology, 48,* 263–274.

Hasset, A. L., Radvanski, D. C., Buyske, S., Savage, S. V., & Sigal, L. H. (2009). Psychiatric comorbidity and other psychological factors in patients with chronic Lyme disease. *American Journal of Medicine,* doi:10.1016j/j.amjmed.2009.02.022.

Heaphy, E. D. (2007). Bodily insights: Three lenses on positive organizational relationships. In J. E. Dutton & B. R. Ragins (Eds.), *Exploring positive relationships at work* (pp. 47–72). Mahwah, NJ: Erlbaum.

Heaphy, E. D., & Dutton, J. E. (2008). Positive social interactions and the human body at work: Linking organizations and physiology. *Academy of Management Review, 33*, 137–163.

Holt-Lunstad, J., Uchino, B. N., Smith, T. W., Olsen-Cerny, C., & Nealey-Moore, J. B. (2003). Social relationships and ambulatory blood pressure: Structural and qualitative predictors of cardiovascular function during everyday social interactions. *Health Psychology, 22*, 388–397.

Horrigan, K. (2010). Beyond sucking it up. *St. Louis Dispatch* (April 11).

Ibarra, H. (1993). Network centrality, power, and innovation involvement: Determinants of technical and administrative roles. *Academy of Management Journal, 36*, 471–501.

Isen, A. M. (1987). Positive affect, cognitive processes, and social behavior. *Advances in Experimental Social Psychology, 20*, 203–253.

Jehn, K. A., & Shah, P. P. (1997). Interpersonal relationships and task performance: An examination of mediation processes in friendship and acquaintance groups. *Journal of Personality and Social Psychology, 72*, 775–790.

Judge, T. A., Thoreson, C. J., Bono, J. E., & Patton, G. K. (2001). The job satisfaction-job performance relationship: A qualitative and quantitative review. *Psychological Bulletin, 127*(3), 376–407.

Kahn, W. H. (2007). Meaningful connections: Positive relationships and attachments at work. In J. E. Dutton & B. R. Ragins (Eds.), *Exploring positive relationships at work* (pp. 189–206). Mahwah, NJ: Erlbaum.

Kanov, J. M., Maitlis, S., Worline, M. C., Dutton, J. E., Frost, P. J., & Lilius, J. M. (2004). Compassion in organizational life. *American Behavioral Scientist, 47*, 808–827.

Karlin, W. A., Brondolo, E., & Schwartz, J. (2003). Workplace social support and ambulatory cardiovascular activity in New York City traffic agents. *Psychosomatic Medicine, 65*, 167–176.

Kelman, H. C. (1958). Compliance, identification, and internalization: Three processes of attitude change. *Conflict Resolution, 2*(1), 51–60.

Kiecolt-Glaser, J. K., Bane, C., Glaser, R., & Malarkey, W. B. (2003). Love, marriage, and divorce: Newlyweds' stress hormones foreshadow relationship changes. *Journal of Counseling and Clinical Psychology, 70*, 537–547.

Kirschenbaum, D. (1984). Self-regulation and sport psychology: Nurturing and emerging symbiosis. *Journal of Sport Psychology, 8*, 26–34.

Knapp, M. L., & Vangelisti, A. L. (1996). *Interpersonal communication and human relationships*. Boston: Allyn & Bacon.

Kok, B. E., & Fredrickson, B. L. (2010). Upward spirals of the heart: Autonomic flexibility, as indexed by vagal tone, reciprocally and prospectively predicts positive emotions and social connectedness. *Biological Psychology, 85*, 432–436.

Kosfeld, M., Heinrichs, M., Zak, P. J., Fischbacher, U., & Fehr, E. (2005). Oxytocin increases trust in humans. *Nature, 435*, 673–676.

Kram, K. (1985). *Mentoring at work: Developing relationships in organizational life.* Glenview, IL: Foresman.

Lawler, E. E. (2003). *Treat people right.* San Francisco: Jossey-Bass.

Lawrence, P., & Nohria, N. (2002). *Driven: How human nature shapes our choices.* San Francisco: Jossey-Bass.

Locke, E. A., & Latham, G. P. (2002). Building a practically useful theory of goal setting and task motivation: A 35-year odyssey. *American Psychologist, 57,* 705–717.

Losada, M. (1999). The complex dynamics of high performance teams. *Mathematical and Computer Modeling, 30,* 179–192.

Losada, M., & Heaphy, E. D. (2004). Positivity and connectivity. *American Behavioral Scientist, 47,* 740–765.

Lutz, A., Slagter, H. A., Dunne, J. D., & Davidson, R. J. (2008). Attention regulation and monitoring in meditation. *Trends in Cognitive Sciences,* doi:10.1016/j.tis.2008.01.005.

Lyubomirsky, S., King, L., & Diener, E. (2005). The benefits of frequent positive affect: Does happiness lead to success? *Psychological Bulletin, 131,* 803–855.

March, J. G., & Simon, H. A. (1958). *Organizations.* New York: Wiley.

Marcus, B. W. (2005). *Competing for capital: Investor relations in a dynamic world.* New York: Wiley.

Mathieu, J. E., & Zajac, D. M. (1990). A review and meta-analysis of the antecedents, correlates, and consequences of organizational commitment. *Psychological Bulletin, 108,* 171–194.

McCraty, R., & Childre, D. (2004). The grateful heart. In R. A. Emmons & M. E. McCullough (Eds.), *The psychology of gratitude* (pp. 230–255). New York: Oxford University Press.

McCullough, M. E., Emmons, R. A., & Tsang, J. (2002). The grateful disposition: A conceptual and empirical topography. *Journal of Personality and Social Psychology, 82,* 112–127.

McCullough, M. E., Pargament, K. I., & Thoreson, C. (2000). *Forgiveness: Theory, research, and practice.* New York: Guilford Press.

Medalie, J. H., & Goldbourt, U. (1976). Angina pectoris among 10,000 men: Psychological and other risk factors as evidenced by a multivariate analysis of a five year incidence study. *American Journal of Medicine, 60,* 910–921.

Mowday, R. T., Steers, R. M., & Porter, L. W. (1979). The measurement of organizational commitment. *Journal of Vocational Behavior, 14,* 224–247.

Niiya, Y., & Crocker, J. (2008). Mastery goals and contingent self-worth: A field study. *International Review of Social Psychology, 21,* 135–155.

O'Reilly, C. A., & Chatman, J. A. (1996). Culture as social control: Corporations, cults, and commitment. In B. M. Staw & L. L. Cummings (Eds.), *Research in organizational behavior* (vol. 18, pp. 157–200). Greenwich, CT: JAI Press.

Owens, B., Baker, W., & Cameron, K. (2011). Relational energy at work: Establishing construct, nomological, and predictive validity. Presented at the Academy of Management Meetings, San Antonio, Texas.

Parsons, T. (1951). *The social system*. Glencoe, IL: Free Press.

Pennebaker, J. W. (2002). What our words say about us: Toward a broader language of psychology. *Psychological Science Agenda, 15*, 8–9.

Peterson, C., & Seligman, M. E. P. (2004). *Character strengths and virtues*. New York: Oxford University Press.

Polodny, J. M., Khurana, R., & Hill-Popper, M. (2005). Revisiting the meaning of leadership. *Research in Organizational Behavior, 26*, 1–36.

Powley, E. H. (2005). *Connective capacity in organizational crisis: Mechanisms of organizational resilience*. Unpublished doctoral dissertation, Case Western Reserve University, Cleveland, Ohio.

Pratt, M. G., & Ashforth, B. E. (2003). Fostering meaningfulness in working at work. In K. S. Cameron, J. E. Dutton, & R. E. Quinn (Eds.), *Positive organizational scholarship* (pp. 309–327). San Francisco: Berrett-Koehler.

Pratt, M. G., & Dirks, K. T. (2007). Rebuilding trust and restoring positive relationships: A commitment-based view of trust. In J. E. Dutton & B. R. Ragins (Eds.), *Exploring positive relationships at work* (pp. 117–136). Mahwah, NJ: Erlbaum.

Quinn, R. E. (2004). *Change the world*. San Francisco: Jossey-Bass.

Rhoades, L., & Eisenberger, E. M. (2002). Perceived organizational support: A review of the literature. *Journal of Applied Psychology, 87*, 698–714.

Riley, S. (1998). *Critical thinking and problem solving*. Upper Saddle River, NJ: Prentice Hall.

Roberts, L. M. (2007). From proving to becoming: How positive relationships create a context for self-discovery and self-actualization. In J. E. Dutton & B. R. Ragins (Eds.), *Exploring positive relationships at work* (pp. 29–46). Mahwah, NJ: Erlbaum.

Roberts, L. M., Dutton, J. E., Spreitzer, G., Heaphy, E. D., & Quinn, R. E. (2004). *Composing the reflected best-self portrait: Building pathways for becoming extraordinary in work organizations*. Working paper, Center for Positive Organizational Scholarship, University of Michigan Business School.

Robles, T. F., Brooks, K. P., & Pressman, S. D. (2009). Trait positive affect buffers the effects of acute stress on skin barrier recovery. *Health Psychology, 28*, 373–378.

Rogers, C., & Farson, R. (1976). *Active listening*. Chicago: Industrial Relations Center.

Rogers, C. W. (1961). *On becoming a person*. Boston: Houghton Mifflin.

Rousseau, J. J. (1992). *The social contract and discourses*. (G. D. H. Cole, Trans.) London: Everyman.

Ryff, C. D., & Singer, B. (Eds.). (2001). *Emotion, social relationships, and health*. Oxford: Oxford University Press.

Ryff, C. D., Singer, B., Wing, E., & Love, G. D. (2001). Elected affinities and uninvented agonies: Mapping emotion with significant others onto health. In C. D. Ryff & B. Singer (Eds.), *Emotion, social relationships, and health* (pp. 133–175). New York: Oxford University Press.

Schneider, B. (1991). *Organizational climate and culture.* San Francisco: Jossey-Bass.

Schwartz, B. (1994). *The costs of living: How market freedom erodes the best things in life.* New York: W. W. Norton.

Schwartz, J. (2001). *Dean's lecture series.* Ross School of Business, University of Michigan, January 31.

Seeman, T. (2001). How do others get under our skin? Social relationships and health. In C. D. Ryff & B. Singer (Eds.), *Emotion, social relationships, and health* (pp. 189–210). New York: Oxford University Press.

Segerstrom, S. C., & Nes, L. S. (2007). Heart rate variability reflects self-regulatory strength, effort, and fatigue. *Psychological Science, 18,* 275–281.

Seligman, M. E. P. (1999). The president's address. *American Psychologist, 54,* 559–562.

Seligman, M. E. P. (2002). Positive psychology, positive prevention, and positive therapy. In S. J. Lopez (Ed.), *Handbook of positive psychology* (pp. 3–9). New York: Oxford University Press.

Seligman, M. E. P. (2011). *Flourish: A visionary new understanding of happiness and well-being.* New York: Free Press.

Seligman, M. E. P., Steen, T. A., Park, N., & Peterson, C. (2005). Empirical validation of interventions. *American Psychologist, 60,* 410–421.

Selznick, P. (1984). *Leadership in administration: A sociological interpretation.* Berkeley: University of California Press.

Sherot, T., Riccardi, A. M., Raoi, C. M., & Phelps, E. A. (2007). Neural mechanisms mediating optimism bias. *Nature, 450,* 102–105.

Smidts, A., Pruyin, A. T. H., & Van Riel, C. B. M. (2001). The impact of employee communication and perceived external prestige on organizational identification. *Academy of Management Journal, 44*(5), 1051–1062.

Spitzberg, B. H. (1994). The dark side of (in)competence. In W. R. Cupach & B. H. Spitzberg (Eds.), *The dark side of interpersonal communication* (pp. 137–158). Hillsdale, NJ: Erlbaum.

Spreitzer, G. M., & Sonenshein, S. (2003). Positive deviance and extraordinary organizing. In K. S. Cameron, J. E. Dutton, & R. E. Quinn (Eds.), *Positive organizational scholarship* (pp. 207–224). San Francisco: Berrett-Koehler.

Stone, A. A., Mezzacappa, E. S., Donatone, B. A., & Gonder, M. (1999). Psychosocial stress and social support are associated with prostate-specific antigen levels in men: Results from a community screening program. *Health Psychology, 18,* 482–486.

Suess, P. E., Porges, S. W., & Plude, D. J. (1994). Cardiac vagal tone and sustained attention in school-age children. *Psychophysiology, 31,* 17–22.

Taylor, J. C., & Bowers, D. G. (1972). *Survey of organizations: A machine scored standardized questionnaire instrument.* Ann Arbor: Institute for Social Research, University of Michigan.

Taylor, S. E. (2002). *The tending instinct: How nurturing is essential for who we are and how we live.* New York: Time Books.

Tutu, D. (1998). Without forgiveness there is no future. In R. D. Enright & J. North (Eds.), *Exploring forgiveness* (pp. 351–375). Madison: University of Wisconsin Press.

Tutu, D. (1999). *No future without forgiveness.* New York: Doubleday.

Uchino, B. N., Kiecolt-Glaser, J. K., & Cacioppo, J. T. (1992). Age related changes in cardiovascular response as a function of a chronic stressor and social support. *Journal of Personality and Social Psychology, 63,* 839–846.

Unden, A. L., Orth-Gomer, K., & Elofsson, S. (1991). Cardiovascular effects of social support in the work place: Twenty-four-hour ECG monitoring of men and women. *Psychosomatic Medicine, 53,* 50–60.

Van der Oord, S., Bogels, S. M., & Peijnenburg, D. (2011). The effectiveness of mindfulness training for children with ADHD and mindful parenting for their parents. *Journal of Child and Family Studies,* doi:10.1007/s10826-011-9457-0.

Vannette, D., & Cameron, K. S. (2008). Implementing positive organizational scholarship at Prudential. Ross School of Business, University of Michigan. Distributed by the William Davidson Institute.

Van Reekum, C. M., Shaefer, S. M., Lapate, R. C., Norris, C. J., Greischar, L. I., & Davidson, R. J. (2010). Aging is associated with positive responding to neutral information but reduced recovery from negative information. *Social Science and Affective Neuroscience Advance Access,* doi:10.1093/scan/nsq031.

Walsh, J. P. (1999). Business must talk about its social role. In T. Dickson (Ed.), *Mastering strategy* (pp. 289–294). London: Prentice Hall.

Weber, M. (1992). *The Protestant ethic and the spirit of capitalism.* New York: Routledge.

Weick, K. E. (2003). Positive organizing and organizational tragedy. In K. S. Cameron, J. E. Dutton, & R. E. Quinn (Eds.), *Positive organizational scholarship* (pp. 66–80). San Francisco: Berrett-Koehler.

Weick, K. E., & Roberts, K. H. (1993). Collective mind in organizations: Heedful interrelating on flight decks. *Administrative Science Quarterly, 38,* 357–381.

Worthington, E. L. (1998). *Dimensions of forgiveness: Psychological research and theological perspectives.* Philadelphia: Templeton Foundation Press.

Wrzesniewski, A. (2003). Finding positive meaning in work. In K. S. Cameron, J. E. Dutton, & R. E. Quinn (Eds.), *Positive organizational scholarship* (pp. 296–308). San Francisco: Berrett-Koehler.

Wrzesniewski, A., & Dutton, J. E. (in press). Hidden pockets of good work: The competence in caring by hospital cleaners. *Academy of Management Journal.*

Wrzesniewski, A., & Landman, J. (2000). *Occupational choice and regret: Decision antecedents and their outcomes.* Unpublished manuscript.

Wrzesniewski, A., McCauley, C. R., Rozin, P., & Schwartz, B. (1997). Jobs, careers, and callings: People's relations to their work. *Journal of Research in Personality, 31,* 21–33.

Index

151

Dutton, J. E.
  climate and, 33–35
  communication and, 72, 73, 78
  leadership and, 2, 4, 17
  meaning and, 89, 92
  relationships and, 45–46, 47, 49, 50, 51, 52, 53, 56

E

Ehrenreich, B., 4
Eisenberger, E. M., 28, 42
Elofsson, S., 48
Emmons, R. A., 39–41
emotions
  carrying capacity of, 50
  collective, 34
  performance and, 70
  positive *vs.* negative, 26
  success and, 32
  See also climate, positive
energizers, positive or negative, 53–59
Epel, E., 47
Esterling, B. A., 49
eudaemonism, 3–4
evaluative communication, 78–79

F

Farson, R., 81
feedback
  best-self, 73–77, 127
  negativity and, 57
Fehr, E., 47
Fineman, S., 4
Finkenauer, C., 7–8, 28
Fischbacher, U., 47
focus
  on deficiencies and weaknesses, 75
  problem *vs.* personality, 82

forgiveness, organizational, 32, 36–39, 124–125
Frankl, V., 85
Fredrickson, B. L.
  climate and, 25, 26, 27, 32
  communication and, 69, 70, 72
  leadership and, 9
friendship groups, 51
Frost, P. J., 33–34

G

George, J. M., 4, 26, 73
Gibb, J. R., 78
Glaser, R., 47, 49
goals
  clarity of, 109–110
  types of, 98–99
Goldbourt, U., 48–49
Gonder, M., 49
Goodman, E. A., 107
Goodnow, J. J., 60
Google, 94
Gottman, J. M., 69–70
"Gottman index," 69
Grant, A. M., 52, 85, 88, 89–92, 93, 94
gratitude, 32, 39–42, 41f, 125
Greenleaf, R. K., 3
Griffin Hospital, 11–15
growth orientation, 98
Gwaltney, J. M., 49

H

Hackman, J. R., 4, 94
Hansen, A. L., 27
Harter, J. K., 51, 60, 75
Heaphy, E. D.
  communications and, 65, 69, 71, 72, 73
  relationships and, 45–46, 47, 49, 50

About the Author

KIM CAMERON is the William Russell Kelly Professor of Management and Organizations in the Ross School of Business and Professor of Higher Education in the School of Education at the University of Michigan. He currently serves as associate dean in the Ross School of Business at the University of Michigan and has served as dean of the Weatherhead School of Management at Case Western Reserve University, as associate dean in the Marriott School of Management at Brigham Young University, and as a department chair at the University of Michigan. He also currently serves as a Fellow in the Wheatley Institution at Brigham Young University.

Cameron is one of the cofounders of the Center for Positive Organizational Scholarship at the University of Michigan—a research center focused on the investigation of positively deviant performance, virtuousness, strengths, and practices in organizations that lead to thriving and extraordinary outcomes. He received BS and MS degrees from Brigham Young University and MA and PhD degrees from Yale University. His research on organizational virtuousness, effectiveness, quality culture, downsizing, and the development of leadership skills has been published in more than 120 academic articles and 14 scholarly books.

Cameron is married to the former Melinda Cummings and has seven children.

By Kim Cameron and Marc Lavine

Making the Impossible Possible

Leading Extraordinary Performance—the Rocky Flats Story

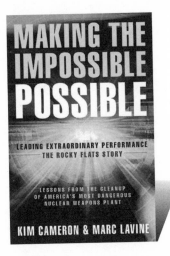

It was initially projected that cleaning up Rocky Flats, the most contaminated nuclear weapons plant in the United States and the site of rampant worker unrest, would take seventy years and $36 billion. But the project was completed sixty years ahead of schedule and $30 billion under budget. Kim Cameron and Marc Lavine discovered that the Rocky Flats leaders used a distinctive "abundance approach," identifying and building on sources of strength, resilience, and vitality rather than simply solving problems and overcoming difficulties. Drawing on firsthand accounts and public records, they identify twenty-one specific leadership practices and techniques that were fundamental to this innovative approach.

Paperback, 296 pages, ISBN 978-1-57675-390-3
PDF ebook, ISBN 978-1-60509-707-7

BK Berrett–Koehler Publishers, Inc.
San Francisco, *www.bkconnection.com*

800.929.2929

Kim S. Cameron, Jane E. Dutton, and Robert E. Quinn, Editors

Positive Organizational Scholarship

Foundations of a New Discipline

Written by internationally renowned scholars, *Positive Organizational Scholarship* is the first collection to explore the dynamics in organizations that lead to extraordinary individual and organizational performance. Just as positive psychology focuses on exploring optimal *individual* psychological states rather than pathological ones, *Positive Organizational Scholarship* focuses attention on optimal *organizational* states—the dynamics in organizations that lead to the development of human strength; foster resiliency in employees; make healing, restoration, and reconciliation possible; and cultivate extraordinary individual and organizational performance.

Hardcover, 480 pages, ISBN 978-1-57675-232-6
PDF ebook, ISBN 978-1-57675-966-0

BK® Berrett–Koehler Publishers, Inc.
San Francisco, *www.bkconnection.com*

800.929.2929

Berrett–Koehler
Publishers

Berrett-Koehler is an independent publisher dedicated to an ambitious mission: *Connecting people and ideas to create a world that works for all.*

We believe that the solutions to the world's problems will come from all of us, working at all levels: in our organizations, in our society, and in our own lives. Our BK Business books help people make their organizations more humane, democratic, diverse, and effective (we don't think there's any contradiction there). Our BK Currents books offer pathways to creating a more just, equitable, and sustainable society. Our BK Life books help people create positive change in their lives and align their personal practices with their aspirations for a better world.

All of our books are designed to bring people seeking positive change together around the ideas that empower them to see and shape the world in a new way.

And we strive to practice what we preach. At the core of our approach is Stewardship, a deep sense of responsibility to administer the company for the benefit of all of our stakeholder groups including authors, customers, employees, investors, service providers, and the communities and environment around us. Everything we do is built around this and our other key values of quality, partnership, inclusion, and sustainability.

This is why we are both a B-Corporation and a California Benefit Corporation—a certification and a for-profit legal status that require us to adhere to the highest standards for corporate, social, and environmental performance.

We are grateful to our readers, authors, and other friends of the company who consider themselves to be part of the BK Community. We hope that you, too, will join us in our mission.

A BK Business Book

We hope you enjoy this BK Business book. BK Business books pioneer new leadership and management practices and socially responsible approaches to business. They are designed to provide you with groundbreaking and practical tools to transform your work and organizations while upholding the triple bottom line of people, planet, and profits. High-five!

To find out more, visit **www.bkconnection.com**.

Berrett–Koehler
Publishers

Connecting people and ideas
to create a world that works for all

Dear Reader,

Thank you for picking up this book and joining our worldwide community of Berrett-Koehler readers. We share ideas that bring positive change into people's lives, organizations, and society.

To welcome you, we'd like to offer you a free e-book. You can pick from among twelve of our bestselling books by entering the promotional code **BKP92E** here: http://www.bkconnection.com/welcome.

When you claim your free e-book, we'll also send you a copy of our e-newsletter, the *BK Communiqué*. Although you're free to unsubscribe, there are many benefits to sticking around. In every issue of our newsletter you'll find

• A free e-book
• Tips from famous authors
• Discounts on spotlight titles
• Hilarious insider publishing news
• A chance to win a prize for answering a riddle

Best of all, our readers tell us, "Your newsletter is the only one I actually read." So claim your gift today, and please stay in touch!

Sincerely,

Charlotte Ashlock
Steward of the BK Website

Questions? Comments? Contact me at bkcommunity@bkpub.com.